NATHAN

The Spiritual Journey of an Uncommon Cat

An Adult Parable... By Jacqueline L. Clarke

D0939683

MAT**U** COMMUNICATIONS

Copyright 1997 ©By Jacqueline L. Clarke

Published by Matou Communications
3153-M Anchorway Court
Falls Church, Va 22042
Fax Number 703 207-3574

ISBN 0-9660596-0-3
Library of Congress Catalog No. 97-92735

There's no such thing as an original idea. Everything in this book is a product of the wisdom of others. I take no credit for these thoughts which might be considered plagiarism if I knew their source. Consequently, I've attributed them to my oldest and most serene cat, Nathan. Unfortunately, Nathan passed away while I was composing his thoughts. But like his life, his death was mostly peaceful. And it is a sense of serenity and peace that I hope the reader finds in these pages.

This book would not have been possible were it not for the unconditional love shown to its author over the years by Nathan, Nestle, Angus, C.J., Billy, Bobby and every other cat I've been privileged to know and love, most of whom have gone on to join their "Higher Meowers." And although each succeeding death has been more painful than the last, it is because each succeeding life has given me an ever-increasing capacity to love.

While my cats collectively provided the character of *Nathan*, the lessons contained herein were learned primarily from the humans with whom I've associated over the past thirteen years -- in the greater Washington D.C. area, Hawaii, and California. I can never thank them enough for giving me the information necessary to change my perspective of life from a problem to be solved to a journey to be enjoyed.

This book is dedicated, with love, to my wonderful Dad, W. Joseph LaCoste.

ISBN 0-9660596-0-3
Library of Congress Catalog No. 97-92735

MATEU Communications, 3153-M Anchorway Ct., Falls Church, VA 22042. Fax 703 207-3574.

Introduction

Mine could well have been the story of a cat gone astray because I was a troubled youth -- first, by my parentage (cars like a bat, feet like a rabbit, angora-tipped whiskers, a tail so long I kept tripping over it), then by my dismal circumstances (living under a dark porch, the smell of the damp earth permeating my coat, dodging stones pelted at me by some little bastard). But I was resigned to my destiny and took comfort in life's small pleasures (a sluggish mouse, a sightless mole, a clumsy, tottering baby bird.)

Life was simple-- not pleasant, but simple. And it could have continued in the same vein indefinitely, were I not lured from my secure cave by the promise of something succulent, unceremoniously snatched by the hairless hand of fate, tumbled into a green plastic laundry basket, and carted off to the bar from whence I got my name.

It was Nathan's bar in Washington D.C. where I met the Hairless Wonder* (The Won, for short) -- up close and personal -- The Won with whom I'd share a house, a much improved standard of living, and a better class of problems. It wasn't easy learning to live harmoniously with myself, others of my ilk, and with alien creatures. But learn I would -- or be miserable I must.

Now, seventeen years later, I'm willing to share what I've learned about living serenely in this strange land -- in hope it is of benefit to man -- and beast. And it is with deep feeling that I can categorically state, "This is dedicated to The Won I love."

---

*The Hairless Wonder's name is derived from his lack of fur rather than traditional hair follicles.

NATHAN
The Spiritual Journey of an Uncommon Cat

Table of Contents

Chapter One

Feeling Better

It seemed like I'd been alone forever under that porch with a dirt floor and cobwebs suspended from the heavy wooden beams above. I was frequently hungry; usually dirty; and, more often than not, a little lonely. My ears constantly itched from the mites and ticks that took up residence in them and I occasionally had other health issues, but life wasn't so bad. I was totally self-sufficient, and the last thing I wanted -- or needed, I thought -- was to be rescued. So when I was forceably snatched from my safe haven and hurled into the unkown, I was so angry I could spit...at least that's how I remember it.

I clawed at the holes in the plastic laundry basket in which I was imprisoned, desperate to escape. But neither chewing nor scratching produced anything other than fatigue. My feelings ran the gamut from fear and frustration to anger. I railed against my fate. "Let me out," I protested over and over again. "I don't want to be here!" I projected what was going to happen next, and it was all bad. (I never knew anyone who projected anything good.) I truly believed, at that moment, that life as I'd known it was over, and I'd never experience freedom or happiness again.

I had no control, no defenses, and nowhere to hide. I felt exposed and vulnerable to everyone and everything...feelings I detested. I couldn't afford to plummet to the depths of despair, so I got angry instead. I was tough. I could take it. They wouldn't break *my* spirit, whoever "they" were. I would somehow escape and find my porch again. All these thoughts raced through my mind in the 15 seconds it took to load the laundry basket into the smelly, careening vehicle that made my stomach feel queasy and the rest of me feel incredibly powerless.

All of a sudden, I was very small and alone. "Why me?" I cried. Why couldn't everyone just leave me alone? I was fine where I was and I wasn't hurting anyone. What was to become of me?

I was so preoccupied with the future that I hardly noticed I was getting car sick in the present. It was a good thing the vehicle soon came to a halt, albeit abruptly, tossing me headlong into the side of the basket which flattened my ears to the sides of my head. After being thoughtlessly jiggled for awhile, I found myself somewhere smokey and dark. It reminded me of my porch. A huge hand then raised the lid of the basket, and plucked me from inside to his chest.

I squirmed, trying to get free; but I was no match for the Hairless Wonder who was holding me by the scruff of my neck. I must have looked like I just had a very bad facelift, with my skin stretched tightly over my skull, the extra flesh bunched behind my ears. Still, that was OK with me. I suspected I was being examined and thought it in my best interest to look as unappealing as possible. I knew there was no use struggling, so I just let my body go limp, hoping he would think I'd been suddenly struck dead. But he took me anyway -- the ghoul -- on yet another car ride that led to a large brick house perched high on a hill.

2

Later, as I was marched through the house, across a noisy tile floor, I thought I detected the sound of running water -- my worst nightmare. Panicked, I kicked as hard as I could to escape, but my back feet were peddling air. I felt myself being lowered, and even though I couldn't look down because of the death grip the Hairless Wonder had on my neck, I sensed what lay beneath me. I made a desperate effort to stop my descent by executing a double leg lock, straddling the sides of the sink. But my claws slid right off the slick porcelain surface which was impossible to grip.

Sheer, unadulterated terror struck as I found my entire body immersed in warm water. Wide-eyed, my heart hammering in my chest, I tried to lull my captor into a false sense of security by pleading for mercy with a pathetic silent meow. Then just as I felt his grip relax, I lashed out, claws unsheathed. I only managed a glancing blow and waited for his violent response; but there was none. I had no choice but to surrender to the inevitable. And just as I stopped fighting, my ordeal was over.

I scrambled from the sink -- talk about walking on water -- and was deposited on a fluffy towel. So relieved was I to be out of the water, I didn't notice the chill in the air until I started shaking like I was doing the Saint Vidas Dance. It suddenly became dark as the towel covered my head and I was caught in a mixmaster of what seemed like a hundred hands all rubbing me in different directions at the same time. Surely, I thought, these indignities must stop...until the next assault was visited upon me...an army of Q-tips invading my ears. "What next?" I whined.

Finally let down on the floor, I was shaken to the core. But my crippling fear was gone. I told my tormentor exactly what I

3

thought of him, my tail whipping up, down, and sideways. But when I looked over my shoulder to witness the devastating effect of my anger on him, he was nowhere in sight.

I turned my attention to some important reconnaissance, finally discovering a toasty spot in front of a hot air vent where I regrouped and thought about what to do next. (I'd always been a master at thinking my way out of tight situations.) But the more I thought, the more muddled I became, until a nap seemed like the best idea. And just as I was ready to slip away, I was taken once again by force, this time into the kitchen -- to be further brutalized, I was sure. But instead, I was gently placed in front of a double dish that contained a snack of milk and a mysteriously mushy, but tastey repast. I had to concede that these victuals beat my usual diet of moths, moles, and other lesser forms of life.

Maybe this isn't going to be so bad, I thought, as I re-evaluated my situation. Physically, I was feeling much better than I had in a long time -- warm, clean, belly comfortably full. And this battle of wills wasn't like a cat fight, after all, where you fought until you'd either won or lost. Surrendering, in this case, didn't mean losing; it just meant I didn't have to fight anymore. Less anxious, but still cautious, I sauntered back into the living room, pausing now and then with my nose to the floor to search out threatening smells. When I didn't find any, I returned to the warm, air-breathing vent, and curled myself into a tight ball.

With one eye open, I could see into the kitchen where the Hairless Wonder (whom I had decided to call "The Won" for short) was mopping up around the sink. He didn't seem quite as intimidating now -- perhaps because his size rather than his

4

demeanor frightened me, and I was getting used to his size. My whole body fit into the palm of his hand, and I knew he could break me in two with one quick snap if he wanted. Somehow, though, since he hadn't tried to hurt me or retaliate for my vicious attack on him when I was trying to escape my bath, I knew he never would. And his size made him a fearsome ally.

I thought about my porch and felt a twinge of home-sickness. That orange tabby, whom I called the Yellow Peril, had probably moved into my spot by now, pissing all over the rafters to mark my territory as his. I was siezed by jealousy and anger at the injustice of the situation. I'd successfully fought him off a dozen times to protect my home -- now I didn't even know where that home was.

Agitated, I licked and licked at my wet fur, but something was different. It felt strange not to taste dirt on my tongue or to struggle pulling out mats of fur. I noticed that my back, which was snuggled up against the vent, was soft and fluffy. And the insides of my ears didn't itch anymore. I wondered, for a moment, if I was getting soft. I didn't want to admit that being squeaky clean on the outside sure made me feel good on the inside.

A part of me was sure that I'd better not get too comfort-able because this probably wouldn't last. Besides, I felt disloyal to my old neighborhood and way of life (despite realizing it hadn't been as great as my euphoric recall led me to believe, but at least it had been exclusively mine.) I was about to drift off again for a short nap, when I felt the floor vibrating beneath me. It was going to be easy keeping track of The Won. I'd always know exactly where he was by the way the floor shook when he walked across it.

I opened both eyes to see him coming toward me and quickly darted under a chair. Playing hard to get, I backed myself as far in the corner as I could, sneezing as a dust bunny tumbled past. (He wasn't much of a housekeeper, I observed.) I saw his large hand groping the dark before he caught my two front paws and dragged me -- and the considerable amount of dust that attached itself to me -- out from under the chair. I didn't like being picked up against my will; but it didn't take a genius to figure out that his will was far greater than mine -- an unsettling fact I pretended to accept with indifference.

I rode high straddling the palm of his hand to another smaller tiled room that was almost too bright. He put me down in a pan of crunchy dirt and proceeded to scratch in it with his forefinger. I was insulted by his obvious lack of faith in my intelligence as he attempted to show me how my new toilet worked. Did he think I was so dumb I didn't know what kitty litter was? I wasn't a rube just because I lived under a porch without man-made conveniences.

The litter wasn't nearly as fine as real dirt, but I knew it would have to do. Anyway, I'd humor him for the time being since my bladder was coincidentally full. I did what was necessary -- threw a bit of sand around with a deft couple of scratches, and hopped out of the box to an approving pat on the head and stroke under my chin. I felt good because my bladder was empty and The Won felt good because I emptied it where he'd wanted. This was my first experience with the fine art of compromise.

I wasn't sure I was going to like sharing my living quarters with someone else, but I had only two choices: try it or cut and run

6

at the first opportunity. Remembering one of the first lessons my mother taught me, "It's always easier to ride the horse in the direction that it's going," I decided to try living with The Won for awhile. Nonetheless, I spent an inordinate amount of time that first week resisting the inevitable -- change. I hid from The Won under chairs, sofas, beds, or anything else that provided a dark (and dusty) sanctuary. It wasn't that I was afraid of him or angry at him. I just needed a temporary escape -- time alone, time to adjust.

I liked my new-found safety and the security represented by "my dish," located by the sink in the kitchen and perpetually filled with sustenance. I appreciated not having to spend most of my time looking over my shoulder for natural enemies or hunting for food, like I did when I lived under the porch. Yet, I felt uneasy and guilty about my good fortune. And, truth be told, I also missed the sport of the hunt and the adrenalin rush of living on the edge. So my feelings about being taken care of, at the expense of doing what I wanted to do when I wanted to do it, bordered on neurotic ambivalence. But that wasn't new for me. When I was here, I always wanted to be there...until "there" turned into "here," then I'd want to be "there" again.

As the weeks went by and I grew more comfortable with my improved circumstances, I came to believe that I had always deserved a better place to live than under that smelly old porch. My self image was on the rise and I, quite naturally, began to take The Won and my better class of problems for granted. As my memories of the porch faded with the passage of time and I forgot the humble beginnings from whence I came, I began to expect the special treatment I was now afforded.

7

The Won liked having me around, and why shouldn't he? I *was* special! Although his demonstrative nature annoyed me at first, I let him pick me up, stroke me and pet me. It actually felt pretty good. And if it made him happy, why not? He must have been a very lonely guy before I came into his life, rattling around in that big house all by himself.

Every once in awhile I would intentionally do something to amuse him, like dance down the corridor on my hind legs feigning a hostile confrontation with an invisible enemy, or grab him around the ankles with my front paws as he walked by. I knew I didn't have to entertain him. All that was really required of me was to lie around looking cute. But occasionally I liked to exceed others' expectations of me. Besides, when I made The Won happy, he made me happy -- by giving me extra treats.

I enjoyed being in the warm house instead of out in the January cold, but I missed the bird pouncing and squirrel chasing. I wondered if I'd ever again feel the thrill of victory, as I tore up a tree after a woodpecker, splintering the bark during the chase -- or the agony of defeat, as I watched it fly away, barely out of my reach.

Then, just as the temperature turned a little warmer, The Won did something totally unexpected. He opened the front door of the house and invited me out. This was an incredible act of faith on his part. I could have just trotted off into the sunset, never to be seen again (the mere thought of which now almost scares me.)

I was understandably hesitant to leave the new-found security of my home, but I rationalized my anxiety with the lame

8

excuse that I didn't want to appear too eager, and thus hurt The Won's feelings. I couldn't imagine to what The Won attributed my reluctance, but if he thought I was afraid of getting lost, he was sadly mistaken. I'd already peed in almost every room of the house, unbeknownst to him, so I could follow my scent home from quite a distance. And I fully intended to do the same around the outside of the house. This time-honored tradition of marking one's territory was another lesson learned at my mother's paw.

I danced around the door stoop for another few minutes. I was unaccustomed to such indecision -- my usual behavior was more like Ready, Fire, Aim! So it seemed forever before I took the plunge and dashed out the door. Looking back at The Won to make sure he hadn't changed his mind, my heart caught in my throat as I saw the unmistaken look of love in his eyes. But I shouldn't have been surprised by his feelings -- or mine. Mother told me that once you slept with someone, the intimacy of the act elevated the relationship to a much higher emotional plane. And we'd been sleeping together every night for weeks. He'd already shown me that he cared for me, and I was a reciprocal kind of cat. So when I left the house, I knew I'd return -- to continue to make The Won's life a little more extraordinary. And by the look in his eyes, I knew he knew that, too.

In retrospect, accepting the things I couldn't change had never been my forte. So why I so readily adjusted from a solo life to harmonious living with The Won was a mystery to me -- one that probably had something to do with grace.

Chapter Two

Flashback

Camped on The Won's chest, rising and falling with the rhythm of his breathing, I felt inexplicably grateful for my circumstances. How did a porch rat like me get here from there -- suddenly a domestic home-dweller -- me, who started life the restless, irritable and discontented product of my mother, "Runaway Sue," and my father, a travelling man.

My mind drifted back in time...I was born *cool -- too cool.* While the rest of my siblings were literally sucking up to Runaway Sue, I sat back contemptuously observing their dependent behavior. I sensed her approval of my free spirit right away. She didn't want to be there either, I thought. I knew, even at that early age, she disliked anyone leaning on her and cramping her style. And she proved my point time and again when she'd bolt from beneath the porch the instant she was done with our feeding, free to roam the neighborhood, leaving me and the rest of the litter to wonder if and when she'd be back. They meowed and whined when she left, but I was stoic, *cool.* And I wanted to be just like Runaway Sue: tough, adventurous, and independent, with my only regard getting what I wanted when I wanted it.

While my siblings cuddled together in a corner of the porch sleeping most of the time, I restlessly combed the earthen floor for signs of life, curiously observing every bug and worm I could find, until that became as exciting as watching a golf tournament. What really attracted me was the sunlight outside. And I knew the very first time I peaked my head out and felt its warmth, that I would spend as much time basking in it as Runaway Sue. Besides, "outside" was where adventure and bigger game were found. I knew this to be true because Runaway said so. And I believed everything Runaway said. (And she was right; my new favorite pastime -- mouse soccer -- was both bigger and better game.)

I never really felt like I belonged to Runaway's litter. I just didn't fit in. And I knew there was more to my being different than the fact that I was grey while the other kittens were black and white. What set me apart was the serious condition with which I was born -- FMS (Fear of Missing Something.) While they were content bonding, busily pawing and licking themselves and each other to feel good, I ran alone and wild, seeking excitement. For me, it was always events on the outside that determined how I felt on the inside.

I quickly became a sun junkie, addicted to the instant gratification of its warmth. Nothing could make me feel better than the sun, and often times I'd just lie down in it anywhere, paying scant attention to my surroundings. After a long nap, I'd awaken with a start, disoriented and wondering where I was. But when my head cleared, I always found my way back to the porch, no worse for wear, albeit a little hungry. I often missed meals because, by the time I got back to the porch, Runaway Sue (still my primary source of nourishment) would be long gone. It didn't bother me to go hungry though -- because I was tough, and I was *cool*.

Besides, I had better things to do. I was going to *be somebody*. So I proved how tough I was by running up to dumb

11

dogs, chasing other cats, battering butterflies, and generally hanging out, long before most of my littermates were fully weaned. I pictured myself in a black leather jacket trimmed with silver studs, collar turned up, lower lip turned down, leaning against a telephone pole -- so *cool*. All the other animals in the 'hood knew me, of course and never failed to acknowledge me. I liked to think I was popular and had a passport to run with any group; but, in reality, I was peculiar and didn't belong to any of them.

As my siblings and I got older, Runaway Sue was around even less. I admired her "chutzpah." She had the most amazing stories to tell about her adventures in the realm of the unconventional. And, although I missed her while she was away, I also understood that a cat had to do what a cat had to do. While the others whined at her, I curled up at her feet and lapped up everything she said. So it wasn't surprising that I was her favorite. She was so very wise!

Despite my youth, she started taking me places to meet her friends, proudly introducing me as her son. (I later learned that Runaway Sue was a little "long of tooth" to still be producing litters, so it improved her image considerably to annonce a new offspring.) I also learned that her wide assortment of acquaintances were mostly ex-mates and half siblings of mine. It was indeed a small world! I seemed to be related to every other cat on the block. She certainly was a free spirit -- actually a little too free and easy, I thought. I worried that her promiscuity might prove fatal; and she was my meal ticket, after all.

One day I decided to "tail" her, following at a safe distance, just to see where she went and whether I could go undetected for a whole day. The adventure was fascinating. After feeding us under the porch, she set out into the sunshine, tail held high in the air.

Her first stop was a small white house with a back porch similar to the one we lived under, only this back porch was filled with bikes, toys, and clutter -- evidence that the house was inhabited by a large family. Runaway Sue boldly marched to the back door and began meowing shamelessly in a loud, pleading tone while she stared at the doorknob with such intensity I thought it would melt. Then, just as though she had willed it to happen, the door suddenly swung open and a human stepped out, scooping up Runaway Sue in her arms and cooing at her.

I watched wide-eyed as the woman petted her, scratching her under the chin until Runaway was purring orgasmically (but she was faking it. I could tell). Then the woman put her down in front of a bowl of milk which Runaway lapped up in a few minutes. I was still hiding behind the bush when Runaway casually strolled inside at the woman's invitation. I waited for what seemed like hours until Runaway reappeared on the back porch, stretching as though she'd just awakened from a most satisfying sleep. She looked absolutely sloe-eyed and so content that I expected her to light a cigarette. I'd almost fallen asleep myself waiting for her, and probably would have, had it not been for sheer willpower and the diversion of a furry caterpillar which rolled itself into a tight ball whenever I nudged it.

Runaway Sue was quick, and I had to really "pick 'em up and put 'em down" to keep pace with her long strides. She chased birds, squirrels and her imagination for another couple of blocks before alighting on yet another back porch. She repeated her first routine, meowing loudly while staring intently at the doorknob, and sure enough, she met with the same result. The door finally opened, another human emerged with a bowl of food, and Runaway Sue enjoyed her second meal of the morning. Once again, she was invited into the house, stayed an hour or so, and re-emerged stretching.

When Runaway repeated this pattern yet a third time, my respect for her knew no bounds. She couldn't possibly still be hungry! It was apparent she was enjoying more than her share of "three hots and a cot" each day, so she must be merely keeping her options open. It appeared to me that half the city thought Runaway Sue was their very own cat and assumed responsibility for her well being. (No wonder she was getting a little pudgy!) And thus I learned what material rewards awaited *me* if I purred a lot and let everyone think that *I* was their very own. (It wasn't until much later that I discovered there was a price to pay for this deceit. Like the phrase implies, "A woman who marries for money, earns every penny of it.")

As Runaway Sue got closer to home, I began to recognize the neighborhood and raced as fast as I could to beat her there. I didn't want her to know that I'd been out from under the porch, much less "tailing" her all day. And I couldn't wait to tell my siblings what I'd learned. I really enjoyed "one-up-man-ship," especially when it was over such a bunch of fur-balls!

But when I ducked under the beam, dashed through the low-hanging cobweb, and romped across the dirt, I came to a screeching halt. I didn't see them; their usual place was vacant.

14

They had to be around here somewhere, I thought, as I let my eyes adjust to the darkness. When I scanned the area and still didn't see them, my initial annoyance was overtaken by heart-pounding fear. Enveloped by a sense of impending doom, I raced from one end of the porch to the other, methodically searching everywhere they could possibly be. But it was no use. They were gone. And their disappearance, I was sure, was my fault. If I'd stayed home where I belonged, I could have taken care of them. I was devastated and instantly filled with shame, guilt, and remorse. By the time Runaway Sue got home, I was panicked enough to confess everything.

She listened patiently as I breathlessly hiccophed my way through my story. Then instead of swatting me with an open paw, like I thought she would, she affectionately nuzzled me instead, assuring me everything would be all right. This made me feel even worse, if that was possible.

Embarking on her own search for the litter, nose to the ground, she swept the area alternately smelling and calling ... smelling and calling. But my littermates were nowhere to be found. I felt numb! Truthfully, we weren't very close, but they were family, after all. And I knew I would really miss them, given time. (I never experienced appropriate feelings concurrently with events. I seemed to have a built-in lag time of a few days to a few months before my emotions caught up with the circumstances that evoked them. No wonder I was always so screwed up! At the moment, I didn't know what I felt -- except possibly relief that Runaway wasn't blaming me for the litter's disappearance. She didn't have to. I already felt badly enough blaming myself!)

15

Runaway Sue was sad. I could tell, even though she tried to hide that fact from me. But her drooping tail gave her away as she kept returning to the spot where my siblings usually slept, evidence of her denial. Then I watched her anger grow as she pushed around huge rocks and pieces of wood with incredible strength, before finally laying down, paws over her eyes, emotionally exhausted. By the next morning she seemed more herself. (There was a part of Runaway, I was sure, that was relieved to be free of the responsibility of kittens.) It was clear she'd adjusted to the situation when she began rationalizing that the others had probably been taken away by some caring humans who'd give them good homes. I couldn't tell if she really believed what she was saying. I didn't -- not for one minute -- even though I desperately wanted to believe. But I kept my opinion to myself, glad that at least *she* felt better. Personally, I was still racked by guilt and the certainty that their disappearance was all my fault.

Runaway stayed unusually close to home for a day or two, but it wasn't long before she acted as though nothing had happened. She certainly was resilient! I was less so, feeling fear and anxiety for the first time in my life -- feelings I dared not share with someone who seemed immune to feeling anything at all. If something bad could happen to my siblings, I reasoned, something bad could also happen to me. I didn't know how to make friends with that particular fear, so I stayed under the porch and just waited for Runaway to come home every night -- hating myself for demonstrating the same sick dependence on her that I'd always criticized my siblings for having.

Then, when Runaway failed to return one night, I dealt with that the only way I knew how. I rationalized. I convinced myself it

16

was sort of a compliment, in a way -- that she didn't feel it necessary to race home anymore because she trusted me enough to stay by myself. But all the rationalizing in the world didn't help when she still hadn't come home three nights later. I couldn't stay curled in a fetal position forever, hiding from the rest of the world. I knew I had to do something. So, I finally overcame my emotional paralysis and went out looking for her.

I prowled the neighborhood searching for the houses she'd visited the day I followed her, but I couldn't find any of them. I really hadn't been paying close attention to where we went that day, and by now there wasn't a trace of her scent left to follow. Occasionally, I ran up to total strangers impatiently describing Runaway and asking if they'd seen her; but they all backed away from me. How crazed and angry I must have seemed! They probably thought me rabid! It never occurred to me to politely introduce myself before asking for their help -- much less to say thank you afterwards, whether I received any help or not.

Returning every night to the spot under the porch that I called home, I'd again curl up in a fetal position as tightly as I could...willing and wishing her to reappear...almost believing I could hear her calling my nickname: Tough Stuff. I continued to desperately hope every night that she'd return, knowing that she probably wouldn't, but being disappointed anyway. Unfortunately, I was right; Runaway Sue never did come home again. And I never knew such pain! I just wanted to die.

I managed to get through the days OK, but the nights were hard. I amped my bad feelings over Runaway by reliving the disappearance of the litter. If I'd had country music to play, I would

17

have used that as a hammer to pound myself further into depression, a state I finally achieved anyway by projecting I'd be alone for the rest of my life. I wasn't accustomed to wallowing in self pity, albeit justified self pity, but I must have liked it because I did it for weeks. (I was to learn much later that depression is often a natural part of the grief process. But there's a big difference between healthy grief and self pity. When you experience healthy grief, you grieve over the loss of another in your life. When you experience self pity, you use that loss as an excuse to grieve over your entire life.)

By the end of the month, I was a mess, having done a good deal of projectile crying. Gone was the devil-may-care attitude upon which I'd prided myself -- I experienced either total despair or an unshakable resolve to never let anyone hurt me again. In either case, I couldn't seem to generate enough momentum to leave my dark, dank surroundings. When I think about that miserable month, I realize how fortuitous it was that I was so totally alone -- because it made me vulnerable enough to lapse into the crying jag that attracted the attention of my captor. I used to think that my "rescue" by the humanitarian who carried me to The Won in that plastic laundry basket was a coincidence -- until someone told me that coincidences were God's way of acting anonymously.

I was quite ready to build a wall around myself, insulated with hurt and anger. But before I could complete the construction, a more potent feeling -- fear -- interceded. I was as terrified of being taken away from my familiar porch as I was of having to spend the rest of my life alone under it. So, the saving grace of my capture was that it interrupted the process by which my sorrow was fast turning to bitterness.

18

I knew I wasn't the cause of Runaway leaving; but I didn't think I was worth staying around for, either. And although I intellectually knew I bore no responsibility for my siblings' fate, there was still a secret place in my heart that felt their disappearance was my punishment for all the bad things I'd ever done. In those days I thought a lot *about* myself, but I didn't think very much *of* myself. Otherwise, I would have been more charitable.

Chapter Three

Trust and the Early Years

My whiskers standing at attention and my nose raised in the air, savoring the smell of the great outdoors, I shook myself back into the present. Casting a glance over my shoulder at The Won still standing in the doorway, I thought about my "capture" months before and how desperately I had wanted to "escape." Now here I was with every opportunity to leave, and I was perfectly content to stay.

I liked roaming around and returning to the sanctuary of my new home. I'd heard about cases where an animal's spirit had been "broken" and wondered if that's what was happening to me. But I dismissed the thought almost as soon as it entered my mind. Why shouldn't I be content? The Won was a decent sort whom it hadn't taken long to train. And to be truthful, he had always been decent to me from the very start. The only thing that had changed about my circumstances was my perception of them.

I realized that escaping or running away was never really an issue -- the issue was having the option to leave, should I wish to exercise it. So with my ability to wander at will, I was, at last, a happy camper. Sure, I still had a wish list as long as my arm. But I was beginning to understand that happiness wasn't having what I wanted, but rather wanting what I had. And I conceded to having the best of both worlds -- The Won was giving me room to roam, yet I had a warm, clean house and a full dish awaiting my return.

As a result of being hungry much of the time as a kitten, I still didn't fully trust that my dish in the kitchen would be filled whenever I was hungry -- despite my experience to the contrary every single day. I guess I lacked faith. So, I occasionally found it necessary to "test" The Won to see if I could make him fill my dish when *I* wanted rather than when *he* wanted . I'd stand in front of him in the kitchen, suck in my cheeks, then drop to my side with a thud. And, sure enough, every time I performed this act of "humility," my dish was refilled. (I should explain that I viewed this ritual as an act of humility because it concerned self-reliance -- not an act of humiliation which concerns self-esteem. Since I couldn't open the catfood cans myself, there was nothing demeaning about asking The Won to feed me. Besides, manipulating him actually improved my self-esteem by making me feel superior and in control.)

The sight of a squirrel caught my eye, interrupting my reverie. I found myself instinctively propelled towards it, racing across the lawn like in days of old. I was in my element as I bounded up the tree after it (thankful The Won didn't believe in declawing). The squirrel was faster than me -- some things never changed -- and I accepted it -- a sign of maturity. I wasn't even disappointed it got away, because the fun was in the chase. And to be truthful, I wasn't sure what I'd do if I every actually caught one.

Squirrel chasing often posed a major dilemma for me, mostly centering around how to return to earth from atop the towering tree I'd climbed in hot pursuit. I naturally thought I could count on The Won to come up and fetch me if I meowed pitifully enough, but he wouldn't. I had no way of knowing that he'd been there and done that before. It seems I wasn't his first cat, nor his first high-altitude rescue. He'd actually accomplished quite a few, before a friend pointed out to The Won that he'd never seen a cat skeleton in a tree. Being unable to dispute that logic, The Won never again attempted, much less executed, such a rescue. So, I'd inevitably have to descend on my own -- ever so cautiously, backwards.

I spent the rest of the afternoon living in the land of "do-as-I-please," annoying birds until it was time to clean out the old intestines with a chaw or two of grass. After indulging in a few satisfying verticle munches, I heard The Won calling from the back door, "blah, blah, blah, Nathan -- blah, blah, blah, Nathan." His language was still somewhat foreign to me. I didn't really understand what he was saying, but I did recognize my name and the tone of his voice. I also knew I'd better go in when he called, whether I was ready or not. If I didn't, he'd be less inclined to let me out on demand the next time. Besides, it didn't matter to me whether I regurgitated the grass I'd eaten outside or on the living room carpet.

Sauntering slowly to the door, stopping here and there to sniff at nothing in particular, I tested The Won's patience. Maybe, because it was my first time outside and he was grateful I actually came when he called (no matter how slowly), he rewarded me with a couple of "Bonkers," my favorite junk food. (I'm sure he learned this elementary behavioral psychology from the pages of *Cat Fancy Magazine*, but that was OK with me. I loved Bonkers and was grateful to get them for whatever reason.)

I strolled into the living room, looking back over my shoulder to make sure The Won wasn't within sight or hearing distance. Positioning myself at the edge of the sofa, I proceeded to sharpen my claws on its nubby surface. If I was truly going to be a creature of the night, I needed to hone my claws to a fine point. And the corner of the sofa was a much better tool for that than the scratching post The Won had so optimistically purchased for me.

I loved the sound of shredding fabric -- it made my coat stand on end. Unfortunately, it had the same effect on The Won! So as soon as he caught me sharpening my claws on the furniture, I'd feign a long, slow stretch before moving directly to the scratching post to demonstrate that I knew the "right" thing to do. (I just didn't have enough maturity yet to *want* to do the right thing.) I was still a bit of an outlaw -- rebel without a claw -- who only *acted* repentent. When I promised I'd try to do better, I knew I was lying before the words left my mouth.

Since I wasn't prone to changing my behavior, I had to become adept at apologizing for it -- and practice made perfect. So, when I knew I'd upset The Won, I'd climb on his lap when he was sitting in his favorite chair and keep nuzzling him until he succumbed to my cuteness. When I'd first moved in, I naively smacked him with an open paw to gain his attention; and he responded in kind. So I quickly concluded that although extending my claws was an effective means of getting his attention, it was not necessarily the kind of attention I wanted.

Living with The Won began to give me a sense of security and "home." And the "homier" I felt, the more possessive and territorial I became about my house and my yard. When I lived under the porch I used to get into fights with the "Yellow Peril" all the time, but those were just to test my emerging "cathood." Now my fights had a loftier purpose -- to protect my turf. I wasn't going to let some other "fish-breath" horn in on my territory. And it was shocking just how much of my time in the yard was devoted to exercising my territorial imperative chasing off other cats, racoons, opossums and squirrels. I knew the latter species were just passing through, so I saved most of my strength for skirmishes with the former -- the real undesirables who'd assuredly cause my property values to plummet, if given half the chance.

The objective of these cat fights was to prove who was "Top Cat" by running him or her (I have to admit, I also fought with girls) off my property with as little physical contact as possible. Like sumo wrestling, much of cat fighting is ceremonial in nature and involves a certain amount of posturing. Holding my breath, I would puff myself up as large as I could, lower my head while humping my back (this is not a easy stance and should not be tried at home), flatten my ears as close to my head as possible, then hiss through my teeth while voicing a gutteral growl that emanated from the pit of my stomach. When my opponent still didn't back off, I'd feign an attack by dancing towards him, stiff-legged, all fours occasionally leaving the ground at the same time, while simultaneously forcing a falsetto scream from my diaphram. If he still didn't back off, I had no choice but to physically attack. I'd ferociously circle the enemy until he or I got dizzy, then launch myself at him with total abandon, missle-like.

Most of these battles took place under our bedroom window and produced an immediate response from The Won, who'd drop whatever he was doing and come hurtling out of the house -- only partially clothed most of the time -- to break up the fight. The Won was very protective and I never doubted his loyalty for a second; but, I also knew he'd do almost anything to save a trip to the vet. His position on veterinary avoidance was a direct result of his financial frugality. He resented any unexpected medical bills, particularly mine -- for lancing abesses that were caused by the bites of my opponents.

If The Won didn't intercede to break up a close encounter before it became a full-scale cat fight, I'd come home looking like an unmade bed and quietly lie in a corner of the house, isolating. Boy, did I hurt! You'd think that after a few fights, all ending with the same result, I'd stop fighting. But part of the insanity of being a cat is doing the same thing over and over again, and expecting a different result. So even though I knew better and always hoped I'd emerge from these matches unscathed, I usually didn't. Thus, I learned (the hard way) to accept the consequences of my actions -- the seemingly endless journey to the sterile, terrifying chambers of my vet.

Neither The Won nor I particularly enjoyed getting there, but at least he didn't get car sick. I did, in between voicing my displeasure throughout the interminable ride. I detest hospitals and the combined smell of antiseptic and fear that pervades them. And even though The Won always took me there in a windowless carrier that inhibited any view during the drive, I always knew where I was the moment we arrived. I'd begin my most pathetic repertoire of desperation meowing , only to be drowned out by the crescendo of barking dogs and screeching cats already in the waiting room (aptly named).

The wait to see the vet was terrifying in itself; but what made it even more so were the screams of the patients being treated in the examining rooms, or the whelps and whines of the persecuted who were imprisioned in the "hospital" out back. (You'd think with all the money vets made, they could invest in better soundproofing.) And, to add to my anxiety, no matter where The Won placed me in the waiting room, my presence was always intruded upon by some overgrown, smelly dog with a wet nose and halitosis -- as if I didn't have enough problems!

I'd scrunch myself into a ball in the furthest corner of my carrier, getting cramps, until it was time for The Won to reveal my cowering presence to the vet in the examining room. I tried to make myself as small as I could before The Won lifted me onto the cold, cold, stainless steel table. I'd go limp with fear, then tense every muscle in my body as I was felt up and down. I didn't even need to see the rectal thermometer to know it was coming. The Won looked sympathetic during the procedure. And, although I knew he was only subjecting me to this humiliation for my own good, it didn't prevent a secret part of me from hoping his next proctoral exam was equally as uncomfortable.

Inevitably, the vet would tell The Won I had a slight fever, lance my absess, give me a shot of antibiotic, give The Won some foul-tasting pink medicine to administer to me at home, then send us on our merry way. I was always so relieved to arrive home after these trips, I'd literally fly from the confines of the carrier as soon as it hit the ground. I'd also promise myself I'd avoid territorial skirmishes in the future. But my good intentions never lasted very long -- after all, a cat had to do what a cat had to do.

I took being a dependent for granted by now -- which wasn't bad, though I feared being lulled into a life of dull routine.

26

Being a pretty spontaneous kind of cat, I hated the idea of living an average life. I had lots of plans for great adventures -- life's little orgasms -- and I wasn't about to concede them yet. It never occurred to me that life was what was happening while I was busy making all those other plans.

So I continued dreaming of far away places I'd probably never see -- and thinking about Runaway Sue, wondering what had become of her. Restless by nature, just like her, my frustration sometimes took the form of plain ingratitude. I could slip into my "Is that all there is?" attitude before I knew it.

I remember waking up on the wrong side of The Won's bed one morning and grumbling while he petted me...muttering while I ate breakfast from my double dish...and sneering at the brightness of the sun as I stepped outside. Sitting in the shade on my deck, listening to the birds chirping overhead, my belly comfortably full, I raised my leg, paw pointing towards the sky, and began washing myself. "Life sucks," I thought, as I surveyed the vast expanse of my yard before taking the nap I'd soon enjoy while other creatures were out hunting for food. When the incongruity of my thoughts and my circumstances struck me, I stopped short, leg still raised in the air, and wondered how I could possibly be so ungrateful? (Few people know that when a cat pauses in the midst of washing himself, leg in the air, he is actually doing some of his finest thinking -- which is comparable to the insights humans seem to experience while in the john.)

It was true things didn't always go exactly the way I wanted, and there were occasional unpleasantries -- like trips to the vet, getting my ears cleaned, and being confined to quarters when

I'd rather be out. But those things were nothing when I kept them in the proper perspective. If I let such petty, inconsequential matters disturb my serenity, it was tantamount to being kicked to death by field mice. I was damned lucky, and most days I knew it. And as soon as I remembered that, my "Is that all there is?" syndrome vanished -- along with all the negative feelings it engendered -- much to the relief of those around me. It was impossible to be hateful when I was feeling grateful.

Chapter Four

Life 101

I always had a tendency to "run to fat," so I tried to impress upon The Won my need for a healthy diet and exercise program. As far as meals were concerned, he was very considerate about feeding me *when* I wanted, if not *what* I wanted.

I've also always been a firm believer in a hearty breakfast to start the day -- even though it was the least interesting of all my meals, because there was rarely anything worth cadging from the table. The Won usually ate fruits and nuts, neither of which I particularly liked. My appetite was more exotic than most, but even *I* drew the line at fruits and nuts -- they made me feel squirrely. So breakfast was just a matter of which flavor of high-calorie, commercially-prepared catfood I'd be served.

I wasn't what you'd call a finicky eater, but I did like an occasional change in diet. And just as The Won thought he'd figured out which brand of catfood I favored (and bought it by the case to save money), I'd develop an aversion to it. I'd wrinkle my nose and curl my lip like I'd just smelled somethig foul (which I did). Then I'd slowly circle the food, before simulating covering it up with imaginary litter (which wasn't easy to do on slippery kitchen linoleum). But I felt it necessary to draw this obvious comparison between what was in my dish and what was in my box, because The Won wasn't a very quick study at times. (And I never wanted to be accused of being subtle!)

I didn't think I had a particularly fickle palate, but The Won was convinced I had an "eating disorder." Changing catfood brands always sent him off muttering to himself that the only certainty about my choice of food was that it wouldn't be what he had on hand. Personally, I thought The Won's real problem was with change...because he resisted it so much.

Being set in his ways, The Won had a totally predictable daily routine. For instance, he always made the bed in the morning right before breakfast. And no matter how much sleep he had or how long he'd been awake, he never failed to bark his shins against the metal bed frame. It never occurred to him to buy a bigger mattress, a smaller frame, or at least pad the one he had. Instead, he'd just rant and rave every morning until the pain subsided.

I'd try to divert his attention by lunging at him from under the covers. But his reaction was never quick enough to elude my claws, which drew first blood and only made him crankier. So I'd retire to the living room with my authentic-fur rodent for a quick game of "mouse toss," or retrieve my well-worn peacock feather for a "drag around" until it was time for a mid-morning nap, followed by a little neighborhood exploration. (Even though I had a much more spontaneous personality than The Won, I was almost as predictable as he, since my routine was contingent upon his. But fortunately my vivid imagination kept my life interesting.)

I always tried to be positive and avoid cynicism; but sometimes it seemed everything pleasurable in life had a price tag attached. My neighborhood outings certainly did, particularly from spring until fall when fleas were attracted to me like flies to cowflops. I usually ended up housing and breeding them until they

30

got bored dining exclusively on me and jumped ship to the shag carpet. When they realized the carpet was an unsatisfactory food source, the fleas, desperate for nourishment, attached themselves to The Won's ankles and other extremities. It always amazed me how long The Won would scratch and complain before he attacked the source of his problem. But when he finally did, he attacked with military precision, detonating powerful bug bombs throughout the house, then fleeing at the last possible moment with me tucked under his arm like a football.

Once the house and carpets were purged of fleas, I'd get a total immersion bath, no more pleasurable today than the first one I was given upon moving in. But I accepted the bath as a necessary consequence of my outdoor lifestyle, another sign of maturity. (Obviously, my perception of my circumstances had changed with time, as well; since, in my best revisionist history, I now believed I'd actually *chosen* to move in with The Won.)

And speaking of moving, I loved to wander the neighborhood and watch the steady stream of people moving in and out on a regular basis. Washington is such a transient town. I had an insatiable curiosity when it came to exploring their possessions, piled high on the curb, under porches and in garages. Since the city is a hot bed of military and foreign service personnel, some of this stuff was pretty exotic. As a matter of fact, I lost the first of my nine lives attempting to appraise an odd lot of household goods temporarily stored in the garage next door. Unfortunately, I wasn't paying attention when the neighbors, who were about to leave town, closed the door of the garage behind them and in front of me. So for days I remained trapped inside, maddeningly listening to The Won calling my name from near and from far -- cursing those

31

neighbors because my predicament was all *their* fault. Frustrated I couldn't get to The Won, nor he to me, I went particularly crazy knowing my perpetually filled dish was so near, yet so far away. But rather than dwell on my certain starvation and death, I chose to sleep most of the time, a very common method of dealing with depression.

Just when I was about to give up hope of ever being found, my mental telepathy finally directed The Won to the garage -- and me in it. The relief he showed upon seeing my repentent face was matched only by my own, which I tried to hide. But when he opened the door, I came flying out of the garage and into his arms, purring so hard I thought I'd choke. I would have been embarrassed if I'd realized how demonstrative I was being.

That was just the first of many times The Won "rode to my rescue." The second of my nine lives was lost only a few weeks later when I discovered I could reach the roof of our house by climbing a rather substantial tree adjacent to it. I loved to keep the "Neighborhood Watch" from my vantage point high above the street -- also an ideal perch from which to snatch birds. On this particular afternoon I was pursuing a small wren that flew under the tent-like chimney cover. Thinking I had it trapped, I dove in after it, only to find myself hurtling pell mell down the pitch black insides of the chimney. Surely, I would have killed myself if I hadn't dug my claws into the soot-covered wall on my descent to the bottom. This maneuver didn't stop my fall, but fortunately it did slow me down enough for a safe landing, feet first, on top of the closed flue. The fall knocked the wind out of me, but I remained miraculously unscathed.

It took The Won too long (in my opinion) to realize I was missing; then even longer to figure out that my cries for help were eminating from inside the fireplace in the living room. But, once again, given enough time and tenacity, he rescued me. And, again, he was so relieved I was in one piece, he didn't even holler at me -- until a day later, after he'd had time to think about it. Then he screamed at my carelessness and promptly put me under house arrest.

I bitterly resented this shabby treatment. Hadn't I been through enough? And I thoroughly resented The Won for meting it out. I spent hours in a corner muttering justifications for my behavior in response to his imagined accusations. Then I remembered another of Runaway's admonitions: "Never argue with someone who isn't there." But I couldn't quite shake my resentment of The Won which tied my stomach in knots. It's odd how resentments work. They're like taking poison and waiting for the other person to die. When I finally conceded that The Won's actions were prompted by his concern for my safety rather than by mean-spirited retribution, I grandiosely forgave him (for his sake) and felt better immediately! I didn't know it at the time, but this was my first instance of finding peace through forgiveness, no matter who was right or wrong.

You'd think I'd be hesitant to go out again after all these fur-raising experiences, but I wasn't. Adventure was what made the world go 'round, and I liked to keep mine spinning. I don't want to leave the impression, however, that my every moment outdoors was filled with adventure. I spent a lot of time just napping in the sun, like I'd learned from Runaway Sue. I found I needed at least four naps a day to sustain me. (Runaway Sue used to lecture me on maintaining balance in my life. She insisted the hours in each day were divisible by three so we could spend an equal eight working, playing, and sleeping.) Since I was fortunate I didn't have to work for either food or shelter, I could devote a full twelve hours to play and twelve to deep, whisker-twitching sleep -- my idea of balance!

No matter where I ended up napping in the late afternoon, I always came home in time for dinner -- The Won's dinner that is. (I had no intention of missing meals like I'd done when I was a dumb kitten.) The Won favored chicken and fish for his evening meal; and, coincidentally, so did I. He was usually good about offering me table scraps, but I usually wasn't very good at waiting for them. I was neither polite nor patient enough to be a gracious dinner guest. Instead, I'd either stare, head cutely cocked sideways, at the food on his fork, paused in mid air, until he couldn't resist feeding me...or I'd hop on the table mid-meal and help myself right from his plate, while his attention was diverted elsewhere. I have to give him credit; he was usually pretty mellow about breaking bread with me. But once in awhile he'd complain that he didn't eat out of my dish, so I shouldn't eat out of his. And when I knew he was serious, I'd carefully back off.

After dinner The Won watched TV, stretched out in his reclining chair, perfectly still except for the jerking of his thumb. Channel surfing to discover what *else* was on TV was his primary source of evening entertainment. He was so addicted to the remote control, his thumb constantly jerked, even when he wasn't holding it. But it didn't matter because, more often than not, the only thing The Won ended up watching in his reclining chair was the inside of his eyelids. (The people who named that chair sure knew how to call a spade a spade!)

But whether The Won slept in his chair or in his bed, my place was always perched atop his chest looking up his nose. I really appreciated these quiet moments together, because my life was otherwise so full. (In retrospect, these moments weren't really all that quiet because The Won snored something awful.)

Every once in awhile I'd open one eye and study his face. I never let him know how grateful I was to him for rescuing me from the garage, extracting me from atop the flue, or just taking care of me. I thought it was apparent how I felt because, after all, I chose to stay with him. (Today I realize that humans aren't that intuitive, so I've learned to express those feelings. I'm shameless when it comes to rubbing up against The Won's leg, nuzzling his chin, and even occasionally licking his face -- when he's sleeping, of course. But back then I wouldn't have risked showing my feelings -- even if I had been aware of them.)

My greatest strength, self reliance, was also my greatest handicap, especially in a shared living situation. Even though I was beginning to trust The Won and feel true affection for him, it was still hard to rely on anyone other than myself -- much less appropriately demonstrate my feelings. I admit I was emotionally challenged, a true beginner at this feelings business. So, I was glad my exposure to others was limited. The Won was in a class all by himself when it came to being the object of my affections -- but that was soon to change when BR entered the picture and my life.

Nathan consulting with his mentor, BR.

Chapter Five

The Mentor

I never had a lot of friends in the neighborhood because I relegated all creatures to either one of two categories: predator or prey. Then, quite by accident, I stumbled upon a very special friendship -- a friendship that changed my life.

His name was Bunny -- Bunny Rabbit -- and he lived across the street in a cage at the end of the driveway. I wasn't sure what sex Bunny was. For awhile, I wasn't even sure *what* Bunny was, or what *sex* was, for that matter. But that didn't stop me from visiting him. Still too young to be prejudiced, I just went with my strongest natural instinct: curiosity.

BR, as I came to call him, was an anomaly to me because all he did was eat and sleep. He never left his cage to hop around his yard, much less explore the neighborhood like I did. (It never occurred to me that he didn't have a choice in the matter.) And he looked different. He had an interesting pointed face; long, long ears; a constantly twitching nose; and bright red, beady eyes. He was also grossly overweight, reminding me of the character "Jabba the Hut" from *Star Wars*.

I didn't know if BR was so out of shape because he didn't get any exercise or whether he didn't get any exercise because he was so out of shape, but that was irrelevant. What was important was that his immobility worked to my advantage. I liked having a "captive" audience, and, I must say, BR was a good listener! I could tell he appreciated my stories because his long ears would stand on end, his nose would twitch with excitement, and his eyes would twinkle with life.

Some of my stories were pretty fantastic -- even *I* must admit -- because I exaggerated a lot to make myself look good. When I told BR about my early days livng under the porch with Runaway Sue and the litter, I implied *I* was their sole support. *I* was the one who went out hunting to provide food for their hungry mouths. *I* was the one who shielded their bodies from the cold. And, *I* was the one who protected my helpless siblings when danger threatened.

My stories were never actually lies, because in order to lie you have to know what the truth is. And I always put a lot of imagination and distance between me and the truth. Being the first born, I always felt responsible for my siblings, and wasn't *feeling* responsible almost the same as *being* responsible?

I loved talking about myself, particularly to someone who never interrupted. I never admitted to being troubled about anything, but when I told BR about a particularly convoluted situation, more often than not, the solution became clear to me. And even when the solution eluded me, the weight of the problem seemed halved just by sharing it. I didn't tell him that, of course. I'd always been a loner, and proud of it!

In one respect, I thought I "knew it all." But in another, I guess I sorely lacked self esteem. BR apparently understood my emotional confusion -- which translated into an attitude best expressed: "I may not be much, but I'm all I ever think about," because he played me like a piano. Early in our relationship, when I shared my problems to either talk them to death or elicit his sympathy, BR assumed a statue-like demeanor of restrained silence. It was only after I began sharing my problems to get his help resolving them that he began offering me bits of his homespun wisdom. He never criticized me or said much, but what he did say was always profound in its simplicity.

I remember what he told me one day when I was totally consumed by the impression I was making on the other cats in the neighborhood. I'd been obsessing about a particularly embarrassing incident for days -- I had fallen and failed to land on my feet. BR studied me for a moment, then said, "Nathan, you wouldn't care so much what others thought of you, if you realized how seldom they did." I was highly insulted by his remark, and didn't return to his cage for a week. But his words were etched into my memory -- to be dusted off in later years when I could appreciate them. Right now, however, I wasn't ready to let go of being completely wrapped around my own axel.

Even the day I went over to visit BR and found his cage overturned, his water dish empty, and food strewn all over the driveway, I could only think of myself. I'd really started to rely on BR's availability, so I was sure something dreadful had happened to him (to somehow screw that up *for me*). I raced over to the cage, which had been covered for the night, dreading what I might find inside. My adrenalin pumping, I pulled back the cover to reveal BR lying on his back, looking like a beached whale. When I knew he was OK, it was hard to keep from laughing.

He explained he wasn't hurt, but had scared himself so badly he'd messed his cage. (He wasn't telling me anything I didn't already know.) He hadn't been paying attention to what he was doing and leaned his full weight against the side of the cage, thereby tipping it over on himself. He felt more foolish than shaken. He told me he'd appreciate it if I could tip it back. Overconfident as ever, my chest puffed with pride, I assured him I'd take care of everything. I spent the next hour pushing and leaning all my weight against the cage, my countenance visibly deflating as I proved I was no match for the task at hand. I was a living example of the difference between humility (acknowledging my limitations) and humiliation (acknowledging them the hard way).

The sight of me (I weighed about three pounds soaking wet at the time) trying to right that cage must have been fascinating, because "The Gang of Four" (neighborhood cats, that is) watched me struggle for quite some time. At first, BR tried to help by shifting his weight around, but it didn't seem as though he was trying as hard as I was -- particularly once we'd gathered an audience. I was beginning to get a little resentful when he finally looked me in the eye and suggested curtly, "Why don't you ask for help?" (I could hear the word "stupid" implied at the end of the question.)

My ears and nose flushed bright pink. "That ingrate," I thought angrily. "He's a fine one to offer me advice. He's the one that got himself into this mess. It would serve him right if I just left him where he is." I recognized my anger for what it was, but never the feelings of inferiority that usually followed. And when I felt "less than," it was natural for me to try to blame someone else for my shortcomings. If only I were bigger and stronger, I could right that cage myself, I reasoned. "It's Runaway's fault I'm so puney. She was never around to properly feed me," I whined.

But, since I had no one to lash out at, I adjourned the committee that was meeting in my head and proceeded with business. As soon as I was sure the others weren't really laughing at me, I accepted BR's suggestion, and invited them to help me. I was so accustomed to the D.I.M. method of problem solving (Do It Myself), that it never occurred to me to ask for help. Wasn't that a sign of weakness? Yet BR had asked me for help when he needed it, and I certainly didn't think less of him, *did I*?

The other four cats and I finally righted BR's cage, and I was surprised by the comraderie I felt while doing it. Those other cats really weren't such bad fellows after all, I thought, pleased with our accomplishment. Maybe it wouldn't hurt to be a tad less self reliant in the future and ask for help when I needed it. (Unbeknownst to me, this was another step toward humility and away from arrogance.)

I felt a little sorry for BR, particularly when I compared his circumstances to mine. I could come and go as I pleased, but he was confined to that cage with no control over his life and no life to speak of. Yet he seemed perfectly content. When I asked him how he could tolerate being a virtual prisoner, he replied that he didn't consider himself in prison. You see, what I perceived as a prison, he viewed as a safe haven -- protection from predators -- and for that he was truly grateful, particularly since he was so fat and slow (my words, not his.) All of his needs were being met quite adequately, he assured me. Then he explained the difference between wants and needs.

41

While I was always searching for something else to fill my life -- new conquests, new adventures, new toys (my wants) -- BR was truly content with his food, shelter, and few possessions (his needs). My philosophy was "more is better." If one of something was good, two were better; if an authentic fur mouse was fun, two guaranteed my amusement. My happiness was always contingent on externals, or getting more things. BR's happiness eminated from within, from the gratitude he felt for what he already had. And because of his "attitude of gratitude," he took meticulous care of his cage and possessions, though they were few; while I was callous and careless with mine. Sometimes I felt ashamed of myself, but I was still young enough to quickly recover from attacks of conscience.

I loved my "cushy" life and wouldn't swap it for anything. But despite knowing I shouldn't have a worry in the world, I was occasionally gripped by inexplicable anxiety -- which BR explained was really self-centered fear -- fear of not getting what I wanted, or fear of losing what I had. And he was right, because my biggest fear was that something untoward would happen to The Won, forcing me to "live on the street" again. If The Won so much as coughed (which he often did as a chronic cigarette smoker), I'd project him dead and buried. And even if it was the middle of a sweltering July, I'd picture myself orphaned and homeless, freezing to death on the steps of the U.S. Capitol.

So the day The Won really did get sick -- felled by a common cold -- I panicked and ran straight to BR to voice my fears. (This was definitely new behavior. But, I must add in my own defense, The Won always overreacted to any malady he suffered, and I was too young and naive to know about

42

hypochondria. So, I naturally believed he was terminal when he said he was.) But once I confided in BR, just sharing my fears took the power out of them

Gnawing on a carrot, BR explained that most F-E-A-R was nothing more than False Evidence Appearing Real. I needed to stop projecting future disaster and live in the present. He suggested I look down at my paws to remind me where I was at this precise moment in time; remember to keep my head where my paws were planted; and talk only to those who were there. If I was successful staying in the "now," I could avoid a lot of perceived problems. Needless worry, he explained, was like The Won paying taxes on money he hadn't yet earned.

If, on the other hand, BR continued, there was real reason to believe that homelessness was imminent, I could start storing food and building a little shelter for myself. This, he advised, was planning -- taking positive action -- as opposed to projecting -- anticipating negative results. And as time passed, I found out just how many of my "problems" never occurred or were actually resolved by staying in the present or doing a little responsible planning for the future.

BR was pretty smart. He could always allay my fears with just a few words. But there was one fear with which he couldn't help, because it was one I couldn't share with him.

You see, I feared for BR's health, because he kept getting bigger and bigger with each passing day -- so big, in fact, he was outgrowing his cage. When the subject of his weight arose, BR insisted that he didn't overeat. He was just "overserved." That sounded like D-E-N-I-A-L to me, which I understood meant: Don't Even Notice I Am Lying.

In my head I knew enough to hope for the best, be prepared for the worst, and ultimately accept whatever happened. But that was easier said than done. Because in my heart BR was as important to me as The Won. And although this feeling sometimes made me think I was disloyal, having them both at my disposal was in perfect harmony with my "more is better" philosophy.

Chapter Six

Relationships

Until confiding in BR, I was totally clueless about adolesence and the bodily changes it wrought. My baby fuzz had vanished along with my baby fat and I was becoming a lean, mean, sex machine searching for a meaningful relationship -- or at least a thought-provoking one-night stand.

Over the past few months, I'd met most of the other cats in the neighborhood; but, until now, I had little reason to care whether they were males or females. Before puberty, they all looked alike. I knew calico cats were always girls, but any other fur-tone could be either gender. And names rarely offered a clue as to sexual identity -- Pepper, Sox, C.J., Midnight, Snowball -- who could tell? So now that I was interested enough to care, I spent a lot of time maneuvering behind my "intendeds" to inspect their fundamental anatomy.

When I told BR about my primitive social skills, he suggested an alternative method for differentiating gals from pals. He advised me to employ all my senses at the same time, including speech -- a novel idea I immediately embraced because I could be far more charming staring into one's eyes than under one's tail.

I didn't feel confident searching for a potential mate beyond my usual radius, so my choices were somewhat limited. I knew other cats threw caution to the wind and strayed far from their normal boundaries in pursuit of passion; but I was afraid of getting lost. (You see, my ancestors ran with the Fugawee (Fu-ga-wee) Indians, a tribe reknowned for hunting, but totally inept at tracking. After a successful hunt, unable to relocate their village, they'd ride to the highest ridge and look out over the plains below, hollering "Where the Fuck-are-we?"-- and that's how the tribe got its name.) I didn't want history repeating itself.

So I stayed pretty close to my neighborhood, in which resided only one female cat. But she met my criteria -- horny and experienced -- so it was love at first sight. Her name was Dolly, and we rendezvoused a couple of times that season. What I liked best about her was her enthusiasm, which seldom faultered unless I got carried away and bit her neck harder than intended. In retrospect, I now see there really wasn't much to our relationship besides sex, but that was perfectly fine at the time.

I didn't know what real love was until I met Kitty. Alas, it was Kismet! I remember it well. I'd left the house in the early morning on a lovely spring Saturday. The people across the street were having yet another garage sale. (It always amazed me how humans cruised around buying each other's junk. It must have been a spring right of passage or a throwback to ancient times when Middle Eastern merchants hawked goods of dubious value in outdoor bazaars.) At any rate, I'd just rubbed up against a rack of dusty and rather tasteless framed pictures and was headed for the card table of assorted kitchenware when I spotted "her." She was coal black, reclining against a tree... legs splayed, washing her flat little stomach. WOW! What a body! What legs! I'd never seen four such gorgeous gams! And that long, pink tongue -- it was enough to drive me crazy! I was smitten. It was love at first sight!

46

I dashed across the yard, tail high, my manhood drafting in my wake. I tried to contain my enthusiasm and stopped short a few feet away from her. (I didn't want to spook her.) As I slowly nosed towards her, closing the distance between us, she finally looked up and spit at me. But even her spit was charming -- a half-hearted hiss. It sounded like she might have a lisp or slight speech impediment.

I was just getting ready to declare my intentions when the slam of a screen door distracted me, and a strange-looking woman with metal protruding from her head flew down the stairs yelling my intended's name. It was Kitty...music to my ears. (At first I thought it might be "Here," but what kind of a name was that?) The woman gave me a disdainful look, scooped Kitty into her arms, and hastily retreated to the house, once again slamming the screen door -- only this time behind them. Patience wasn't one of my strong suits. I wanted everything NOW. But I knew I'd have to wait to meet this sweet young thing -- *my* Kitty. And she would be worth waiting for, I was certain. For now, I'd just have to be satisfied knowing where she lived.

I moped around the house for the rest of the day, my demeanor causing The Won some concern. It was most unusual for me to be at home in the middle of the day, much less watching TV. (I hated daytime television. To be truthful, I didn't think much of nighttime television either. The only show I consistently watched on TV was *Wild Kingdom*, and that was usually re-runs of Marlin Perkins wading through a swamp to capture some pissed-off predator.) But I wasn't actually watching the TV anyway; I was just sitting in front of it, thinking of "her" and picturing our life together.

47

The Won tried tempting me out of my reverie by dangling the feather-on-a-stick in front of my nose, but I wasn't interested. I was perfectly content fantasizing about the happiness Kitty and I would know, and plotting exactly how I would bring it about.

In my head, we'd already had our first conversation, then our first nuzzle. Unable to resist my animal magnetism, she succumbed to my desire. We were now head over heels in love, running slow motion through fields of daisies. And everything was purr-fect -- everything, that is, until she told me she was pregnant. Then she changed. I could never do enough for her. She'd constantly whine and nag at me while she swelled to magnificent proportions. Gone were her girlish figure and soft-spoken demeanor. Now it was painful just spending time with her. "Where was I last night? Who was I with? Why didn't I spend more time with her?" she'd ask accusingly. Now when she spit at me, she really meant it. And the more demanding she became, the more desperate I became -- to escape. I felt trapped and wanted out!

I was close to despair before I remembered I was daydreaming. Shaking my head to clear it, I was relieved to return to the present. Was I crazy? A relationship with that ungrateful bitch was totally out of the question! I didn't need her -- or any female, for that matter -- complicating my life and telling me what to do. Thank goodness I came to my senses before I got too involved. I sighed with relief as I took my feather-on-a-stick to The Won. The familiar was so comfortable.

After breakfast the next morning, I sprawled on the ledge of the picture window, forgetting my former resolve, and stared at Kitty's house. What had I been thinking? I'd never even actually

48

met her, much less given our relationship a chance. So as soon as I spotted her sharpening her claws on the tree in her yard, I decided to rectify that situation. I had a lump in my throat and a tightness in my chest I knew wasn't heartburn; and it didn't take any more than that to propel me into action, abandoning my former resolve to leave well enough alone.

It was only 6 a.m. and The Won wasn't up yet; but whether he knew it or not, he was about to be roused in short order. I tore into the bedroom, leapt onto the bed, and bounded over his prone form. After executing a number of jumping jacks on his stomach, I padded over his chest to the vantage point just below his chin where I could closely watch for eye movement. When there wasn't any, I nuzzled his face with mine. This technique not only confirmed he was still alive and breathing, but also served to tickle him awake. He feigned sleep, thinking I'd go away; but I was tenacious. I kept pestering him, clawing at his hair and chewing on his ear, until he grudgingly got out of bed and released me into the light -- and, more precisely, into "her" backyard.

Our first moments were awkward. We even smelled each other -- like animals. Once that was behind us (literally), I didn't know what to do next. I'd never courted anyone before. Jumping on and off Dolly's bones didn't constitute courtship. I was rescued by a favorite adage of BR's: "When in doubt, nothing is often the best thing to do, and nothing is always the best thing to say." So I excused myself, suggesting we meet again later in the day (after I'd had a chance to solicit some advice from my mentor, my answer man). Fortunately, BR *did* know what constituted a courtship and wasn't adverse to telling me.

49

He said there were stages to developing a lasting relationship. First, there was the companionship stage. You enjoyed doing things of mutual interest together because you had mutual interests in common. Second, was the friendship stage. You enjoyed doing things together because you wanted to be together, and being together was more important than what you actually did. Third, came the courtship stage when you wanted to be together all the time, to the exclusion of seeing others. And last, was the commitment stage, when you decided to be together forever, whether you always wanted to or not, doing the things you *had* to do as well as the things you *wanted* to do.

Unfortunately, I was constitutionally incapable of following BR's advice or timetable in establishing my relationship with Kitty. Remember, I was impatient. So instead of allowing "a meaningful" relationship to develop, I coerced her into sleeping with me immediately -- thus propelling us directly to stage three on our first date. So it seemed perfectly logical to rent that U-Haul on our second date so I could move my feather-on-a-stick and other favorite things to her place.

BR had also cautioned me that the euphoria of an early relationship was primarily hormonal, and not to be surprised if the intensity didn't last. But I didn't want to believe I'd ever lose that soaring feeling I experienced with the first flush of adoration. But, once again, BR was right. The feeling didn't last. And when I started "coming down" from my emotional "high," I missed that feeling of elation. I felt cheated, and blamed her for not sustaining our passion or living up to my expectations. (This occurred on day two.)

Since we'd sacrificed intimacy and communication for pure pleasure, there was no foundation to the relationship and we had nothing to fall back on once the "magic" was gone. As a result, our union floundered and we parted company. I discovered that breaking up was hard to do, just like the song said. And I was hurt and angry -- even though it was what I thought I wanted.

BR tried to console me. He said that relationships were never all black and white. Ninety percent of them were in that vast grey area somewhere between unconditional love and total estrangement. He said that the only requirement for being in one, was the desire to be, and perhaps I wasn't ready. I'd gone from one extreme to the other in record time, I realized; but that wasn't unusual for me. I had no experience with *moderation* -- a point I consistently swung past on my way from one extreme to the other.

Even my life's goals tended toward the extreme. One minute I wanted to be as "rich as Rockefeller," and the next minute as poor and selfless as Ghandi. I could be motivated as easily by greed as by altruism. I could picture myself eating out of a Baccarat crystal dish on the marble floor of the mansion I purchased with my earnings from 9-Lives commercials -- or, dressed in sack cloth and ashes, ministering to the poor, homeless, ferral cats of Key West, Magic Island in Waikiki, and the Colliseum in Rome. But, in either case, my view of my own self-importance was as dramatic as it was unrealistic.

I never dared to be average. As a matter of fact, I was contemptuous of the concept of average. I kept getting "average" confused with "mediocre." I usually felt "better than," or sometimes "less than," but almost never just "equal to." I was

51

either very up or very down, never even. So my inability to exercise moderation or restraint in a relationship shouldn't have been a surprise. Once the bonfire of passion was extinguished, I was out of there! No settling for warm embers or the faint glow of a loving companionship for me.

I did try several other relationships, sure that a "she" in my life was the answer; but none of them worked out either. I kept lying to myself (and to her) about my capacity for a total commitment. When all was said and done, I was still too selfish to put anyone else's needs before my own. BR knew without being told that I had problems -- unreasonable expectations, intolerance, impatience; but my basic problem was self-honesty. And although he tried to help me, I was pretty far removed from putting into practice his definition of honesty: complete harmony of thought, word, and deed. The truth was that I hadn't felt sufficient emotional pain to force me to change or grow. And honesty didn't sound like an ideal whose time was right -- not for me, anyway.

Before jumping into my last relationship, I hoped it would prove to be an experience rather than another lesson. It was an attempt at reconciliation with Kitty, the mother of my litter. I thought I had changed sufficiently to make a go of it. I wasn't nearly as judgmental, consciously making an effort to focus on the things I liked about her rather than the things I didn't. I also tried being kind, but I was still too selfish to actually *be* kind. The best I could do was to *act* kind occasionally. And to no one's surprise but my own, the relationship failed a second time.

Each time a relationship ended, I'd go to BR and objectively detail my mate's character deficiencies so that he had a clear understanding of what I'd been dealing with. I was always careful not to sound too critical, adding "Bless her heart" after commenting on a particular shortcoming. But BR wasn't fooled; he exposed these attempts at character assassination for what they were. When I'd try to argue in my defense by rebutting one of his observations, he'd stop me dead in my tracks by saying "Nathan, everything after but is bullshit." He'd then counsel me that instead of belittling someone, I should try to transform myself into the creature I wanted them to be -- a suggestion to which I didn't have a response.

Finally and reluctantly, I concluded that I didn't need a female to make me feel complete (sour grapes). I could fully enjoy an alternative lifestyle. My relationship with The Won provided me with unconditional love, while my relationship with BR gave me unconditional friendship. And I could go to either of them whenever I felt emotionally needy, I rationalized. What more did I need? All the while, I was still imagining where *else* I could possibly cast my social net to bag the female of my dreams.

Whenever I was alone, I tried to convince myself that I was experiencing solitude, a state of being, rather than loneliness, a state of mind. And often being alone *was* a matter of choice for me; but, on occasion, I was hardly immune to the same loneliness other singles experienced. I realized my desire for a relationship was, in part, socially motivated. But, in truth, I also suffered neurotic ambivalence about that, too. At times I really wanted a her in my life to share a particularly beautiful moment. But if I did have a her in my life, I might not have that beautiful moment to begin with -- because I may not have had the freedom to be where I needed to be, doing what I needed to do, to create it.

Then I spent hours contemplating the natural evolution of relationships within the species. From birth to young adulthood, I had exclusively enjoyed the company of other tomcats; females never entered the picture. It wasn't until puberty that my fraternal instinct buckled under the force of the surging hormones that drove me to seek female companionship. But by middle age, I was sure, my body chemistry would right itself, my primal urges abate, and my good sense return, propelling me back into the company of my brothers -- proving my inital instincts correct after all.

Still, all my rationalizing and speculating didn't make me feel any better. What *did* was BR suggesting that all of our relationships in life are pre-arranged. When I heard that, I relaxed. The heat was off! I would meet my soulmate when I was supposed to, and not a minute before.

As it turned out, I needn't have wasted so much time dwelling on such thoughts, because as soon as I reached full maturity, The Won had me "fixed." (I still blanche at this term which certainly doesn't represent my view of what happened to me.) I did eventually learn to accept my neutering as a blessing, however; since it relieved me of ever again having to choose between sex and serenity -- which were totally incompatible in my case. (BR also made me feel better when he told me that I wasn't unique. "Eventually everyone is neutered. It's just a matter of time before it happens as part of the natural aging process," he said.)

Perfectly content to surrender my former personna of "party animal," I started becoming a more mature community creature -- and none too soon, because that role would soon be thrust upon me with the arrival of new and unexpected responsibilities.

Chapter Seven

Sibling Rivalry...My Side

Once the issue of "relationships" had been settled for me, my life began running like a well-oiled machine. The Won couldn't do enough to provide all my physical needs. BR, always available to lend an ear (two very adequate ones, actually), satisfied my emotional needs. And a plethora of fauna -- everything from rapacious racoons to pesky opossums -- fulfilled my recreational needs.

The only source of potential conflict in my world was between The Won and the two elderly ladies next door who were inordinately fond of birds. While I considered their backyard my private preserve, they considered it a sanctuary for their feathered friends whom they enticed with elaborate feeding stations. Hiding in a flower box below one of those feeding stations, I'd patiently wait for an unwary subject to alight for a snack. Then I'd execute a standing broad jump of Olympic proportions and snatch him right off his perch in mid-peck.

My idea of picking up after myself was to carry the corpse home to The Won, proudly depositing it right on the front door stoop where he couldn't possibly miss it. He always appreciated these tokens of my esteem, I could tell -- unless he accidentally stepped on the dead bird barefooted as he went out for the morning paper.

When I was particularly successful hunting, it wasn't uncommon for me to leave several of my prey on the lawn wearing dirt shirts. If I was lucky, they would be found and disposed of by a yardboy or errant repairman. If not, the ladies would occasionally come upon one of the victims before it had a chance to decompose. Filled with righteous indignation, they'd march over to our house to shake a finger at The Won and make him view the evidence of my trespass and bad character.

Presented with a ruffled corpse, The Won would half-heartedly suggest an explanation for the bird's demise -- heart failure from the stress of city living, or death from eating poison berries. He tried to paint a picture of stricken birds suddenly keeling over in the treetops and dropping like stones to the ground below, but the ladies weren't buying it. Everyone knew I was responsible for the decline in the bird population; and, although this knowledge strained our neighborly relations, it certainly enhanced my reputation with my peers.

Every new conquest was a feather in my cap (pardon the pun), until The Won made me feel guilty and remorseful enough to halt my activities. He explained that hunting for food to eat was OK, but that killing for sport was not. And since I was already well fed at home, I had no business loading up on the buffet of life just to leave it sitting on my plate. He had a point. So, although I still relished the sport, I prudently practiced "*huntus interruptus*."

I even called a truce with the other cats in the neighborhood (as long as they respected my turf). And they usually gave me and my yard a wide berth. This suited me just fine, because I was still very selfish and overprotective of what was mine. I didn't want to share anything with anyone else -- my yard, my hunting grounds, my toys, my friendship with BR, and my relationship with The Won. I felt that I'd *earned* everything the hard way; although in reality, most of what I valued had been handed to me on a silver platter.

I was never more miserable than when I was in the midst of that old self-centered fear, afraid that I wouldn't get what I wanted, or that I would lose something I already had. It had been a long time since I had reason to be fearful -- so long, in fact, I'd almost forgotten what it was like -- until the day The Won came home carrying a rather large, ventilated box from which I heard weak and pitiful meowing. I froze in my tracks, not wanting to believe what I suspected. Could it be? Could it be possible? The box actually contained a rug rat, a sibling, a kitten?

I jumped down from the dining room table where I'd been sunning myself, and waited for The Won to place the carrier on the floor. Sniffing all around it, I almost gagged on the smell of baby powder. If he thought he could hide a kitten from me by disguising its scent, he was sadly mistaken. Besides, that God-awful whining was a dead give-away.

I peeked into one of the ventilation holes to confirm my worst fear. Aghast, I saw not one, but two, round lumps of fur cowering together in the corner of the box. And before I could get a good look at either, one of the little bastards leapt at me, nearly scratching my eye out. I hissed menacingly and backed off, while waiting for The Won to open the box -- from a safe distance. When he did, out spilled two pudgy kittens: one pure white except for orange marmalade markings on his ears, nose, and tail; the other a

57

creamy beige with chocolate ears and tail. They certainly were ugly. Their coats stood on end like porcupines. Their blue eyes looked a little crossed to me. And their noses were so pushed in they resembled punch-drunk pugilists.

I cocked my head and looked solefully at The Won, pleading with him to deny what was apparent. But he obviously didn't feel that he owed me an explanation, which hurt even more. To add insult to injury, he seemed to be protecting them from *me*, his *best* friend. Because when I aggressively danced towards them, intent on displaying my full magnificence, The Won snatched me up and held me away by force. I growled, the sound coming deep from my throat, while staring them down. I was pleased with the effect I was having, until The Won unceremoniously tossed me out the front door.

Now I was on the outside, looking in. (I wished The Won would wash the picture widow. It was hard to see through the spreckled dirt that clouded the glass.) I could barely make out the two kittens rolling around on the floor, chasing their tails, and climbing up The Won's pant leg while the old fool chuckled in delight over their antics. I heard him talking to them in a condescending tone of voice, calling the white one "Angus" and the beige one "Nestle." At least he treated me like the equal I was, I consoled myself. It would be a cold day in Hell before *I* had anything to do with those two. They were obviously in the most obnoxious stage of cat development -- "nutshood."

In disgust, I turned my back on all of them and marched across the street, my regimented pace belying my tumultuous feelings -- which swung from indignation to inferiority. How could he do this to me? How dare he not consult me! What did he need kittens for? Wasn't I enough cat for him? I seethed with anger and jealousy, hating all the changes I was sure were about to take place in my formerly wonderful life. I thought about three dishes lined up on the kitchen floor. The place would look like a cheap cafeteria -- and they'll probably have their noses in mine as soon as I turn my back. My next thought was about my litter box. Damned, I bet they aren't even toilet trained yet. I'd better mark the rooms again before *they* foul them. And I'll draw the line at using the same litter. Either The Won gives me my own box or I'll piss in his shoes! And my toys...what about my toys? They'll have kitten spit all over them!

The more I thought, the angrier I became. I had worked myself into such a state, I found myself madly muttering in front of BR's cage. I guess I'd gotten there by rote. I knew he was awake, despite his eyes being closed, because his lips were moving as he munched the residue of a carrot. And he knew I was angry by my agitated state.

After reminding me that anger is like an acid that eats its own container, he encouraged me to talk in order to get rid of it. I watched the expression on his face for a sign of sympathy as I poured out my heart and soul. When I finished my lament, however, BR merely opened one eye. "Did you ever stop to think that this isn't about you?" he asked. "Besides, look at all you have to gain, instead of what you have to lose." He suggested I focus on the positive. I'd now have three dishes of food from which to choose instead of one; I'd be let out more often since The Won hated to clean litter and knew I preferred using the "outhouse"; and I'd have access to all those new toys bought for the kittens.

Furthermore, BR added, I might even enjoy playing with the kittens themselves. And as soon as he said that, my mind's eye envisioned a number of interesting new parlor games: games like Carpet Bowling, as I rolled them across the floor from one end of the room to the other; Kitten Toss, throwing them as high in the air as I could; and Fur Splat, nudging them off the edges of furniture and watching them hit the ground. I smiled.

By the time I returned home, I was feeling much better. I no longer had a problem, merely a situation with which to deal. But I was still a little miffed that The Won had brought them home without consulting me first, so I continued to give him the "cold shoulder" to demonstrate my annoyance. Too bad I was such a pushover for a good massage. As soon as he lifted me on his chest and began rubbing my back, I emotionally caved in and purred with my former abandon.

During the next few weeks I remained aloof, absenting myself as much as possible to punish them all -- The Won for what I still considered his emotional betrayal, and the kittens just for being alive. I'd leave the house in the early morning, go across the street to visit BR, then meander over to the Murphy house for a little undivided attention. Mrs. Murphy, bless her soul, was a sucker for a furry face, and she loved mine.

As soon as she saw me on her back porch, she'd open the kitchen door, let me in, and graciously offer me some milk. It was true, she didn't have much to offer and her house was smelly and messy, but any port in a storm. All I had to do to stay in her good graces was purr a little, rub up against her leg, and occasionally sit on her lap for awhile to delude her into thinking I was actually hers. I didn't feel the least bit guilty about what I was doing; but it did give me a strange sense of *deja vu*, reminding me of the day I followed Runaway Sue and watched her do the same thing. "It's true, the apple never falls far from the tree," I thought.

I started spending a lot of time at the Murphy house, expecting The Won to be devastated by my rejection, which I now realize he hardly noticed. Sometimes I'd sit under the Murphy's porch until the wee small hours of the morning, spitefully planning my emotional betrayal of The Won until I heard him looking for me, hollering my name throughout the neighborhood. This event usually occurred promptly at 10 p.m. (There was a TV commercial that asked, "It's ten o'clock. Do you know where your children are?" I suspected that The Won's search for me was his knee-jerk reaction to the commercial, since he always looked for me exactly at 10 p.m.) I didn't come when he called, of course. I was still punishing him. But I did make sure I got home at least once a day to remind the kittens it was still *my* home and *my* choice not to be there. Running away from home each day, only to return for dinner each night, was a sensible compromise between drama and practicality, I thought.

On those occasions when I did stay out all night, I'd show up outside the dining room picture window in the morning, watching The Won eating his breakfast until he sensed my presence. He was always relieved to see me. It made me smugly satisfied to know that I'd kept him in a state of high anxiety all night. After I had *my* breakfast, I'd curl up on the couch in the living room, waiting for Angus and Nestle to pay homage -- my due as the oldest and wisest cat -- but they never quite lived up to my expectations. BR'd cautioned me about that. He said

61

expectations were nothing more than premeditated resentments and I should try not to have them. Actually his exact words were: "Nathan, you'll be a lot happier in life if you avoid setting conditions, making judgments, or having expectations."

I preferred concentrating on the kittens' deficiencies rather than looking for any of their virtues. So it was remarkable when I began to notice some development in them -- as retarded as it was. Angus was the talker; he was always yapping, though he rarely had anything worthwhile to say. Nestle was the strong, silent type -- an explorer whose dust-covered head was a dead give-away he'd been poking it in places it didn't belong. They'd never grow up, I was certain. They'd just keep getting bigger.

And physically they were getting bigger; there was no doubt about it. Angus now reminded me of a cute young harp seal (the kind poachers club to death for pelts), while Nestle more closely favored the otter family (he laid on his back so much, I fully expected to see a clam shell between his front paws). God, all these ocean-related analogies were making me hungry for seafood.

I took great delight when The Won yelled at the two of them for openly doing in public what I now only did in private -- like sharpening their claws on the furniture. The Won thought I'd broken this nasty habit as soon as I started going outside; but every once in awhile I'd get a yen for the feel of fabric shredding between my claws and revert to my former socially unacceptable behavior. The boys, as I now called them, could learn a thing or two from me about being circumspect. But they'd have to come to that conclusion themselves.

I often wished I had a cat door in the house so I could go in and out as I pleased without having to depend on The Won for my access and egress. He was getting better at coming when I called, but occasionally he'd be otherwise occupied or ignore my demands to be let out -- particularly if he thought it was too late. I always wondered, too late for what? In any event, his concept of "too late" and mine were poles apart. As far as I was concerned, it was never "too late." That was like being too rich, too thin, or too popular.

Whenever I complained to BR about not getting a cat door of my very own or anything else I wanted when I wanted it -- instead of being sympathetic, he'd remind me, "When you measure your life on the basis of getting what you think you want, you'll always be discontented. When you evaluate your life on the basis of getting what you need, you'll always be grateful." The trouble was, I didn't feel very grateful at the time.

The kittens had been around for about two months when I came home to a bizarre scene! The Won was out in *my* yard, leading the two of them around at the end of a leash. They weren't very bright, as I may have mentioned; so instead of walking with him, they were literally being dragged along behind him through the tall grass. I would have found this sight far more amusing were it not for what it portended: their imminent invasion of my turf, my yard, my last bastion of privacy! Here was yet one more resentment against The Won. But then I remembered how obsessed I became with my resentments. They were a lot like stray cats -- the more I fed them, the longer they stayed around. So I tried reason instead.

I cautioned The Won that the boys were too small to be wandering out there on their own. But judging from his reaction,

63

the same could have been said about his mind, because he showed no inclination to take my advice. So instead of keeping them inside like I suggested, he now had three of us to herd homeward every night. And, quite frankly, he couldn't afford the time. He already had a full-time job tending to our other needs. Everyone's conflicting schedules really required the employment of a dedicated domestic, but I knew The Won was too cheap to ever consider such an option.

Angus was the first of the pair to give The Won and me more grey hairs by disappearing for an entire day. I helped frantically comb the neighborhood for him, but after hours of futile searching, I returned to the house exhausted and collapsed on the living room carpet. As soon as I got quiet, my sensitive ears picked up the sound of scratching coming from inside the fireplace. I couldn't believe it! Angus had taken the same fast track down the inside of the chimney that I'd taken as a kitten. I smiled to myself, picturing our clawmarks side-by-side, descending the entire length of the soot-covered firebrick -- from the top of the chimney to the bottom of the flue. History really did have a way of repeating itself!

In six months, the boys were going through that awkward adolescent stage, and I was spending more time at home with them (mainly because no one missed me when I was gone and Mrs. Murphy was becoming too possessive). I was still Top Cat and didn't let them forget it, forcing them out of my favorite spots both indoors and out. But I was actually beginning to enjoy them -- and, at times, I was even proud of their development under my tutelage! What's more, I was fascinated by their budding personalities. And, to tell the truth, I was more than a little jealous of their closeness -- symbolized by the way they took turns washing each other's faces, for God's sake! It surprised me to acknowledge that I cared about such things, but I was beginning to feel a part of something bigger than myself -- a family.

When it was Nestle's turn to disappear, Angus naturally took it the hardest. The Won and I were terribly worried, of course; although we tried to keep that to ourselves. But when Nestle had been gone for more than 24 hours; and Angus could neither eat nor sleep (and swore he wouldn't until Nestle was found), I sprang into action, expanding the search beyond the usual neighborhood boundaries.

Cleverly disguised as a responsible adult, I set out to find my brother in strange and distant neighborhoods. This was a long, tedious process that required spraying numerous trees and shrubs en route to ensure that I'd be able to follow my scent home.

Threatened by dehydration, I systematically combed each neighborhood and yard, bush and shrub, one by one. And just when I thought I couldn't possibly spray one more piece of vegetation, I sensed movement under a thick privit. Wary it could be a 'coon or 'possum, I approached cautiously. When I recognized the faint meow as Nestle's, I dashed headlong into the bush, pushing aside the branches with my face. And there was Nestle, caught by his collar, only a little worse for the wear and exceedingly glad to see me -- his big brother!

I lectured him all the way home, constantly looking over my shoulder to make sure he was keeping up with me. I was experiencing so many feelings at once...love, pride, anger, relief... I felt like I was going to jump right out of my skin. Rescuing Nestle

65

was such a mature thing to do! BR always told me that being responsible was *doing* the next right thing, while being mature was *wanting* to do the next right thing. Well, I guess I was finally maturing because I *wanted* to take care of my brothers.

I couldn't wait to see the look on Angus' face when I brought Nestle home. And I also couldn't wait to curl up in The Won's lap to share this poignant moment with him. Life was good! As we climbed the stairs to the front door, I anticipated my reward. Maybe The Won would finally buy me that cat door I wanted. He'd certainly be grateful enough, I thought to myself!

I'd been so preoccupied with getting home, I didn't realize it was well after dark until I saw the lights on in the living room. I scratched at the picture window, while peering through it looking for The Won. Gee, he must be in bed already, I surmised when he didn't come to the door right away.

Startled by a sound behind me, I turned to see The Won, clad in his pajamas and slippers, coming up the front steps. I waited for his face to break out into a wide smile at the sight of Nestle and I sitting on the front doorstoop. But it didn't. The original scowl he was wearing remained unchanged. "Nathan Clarke," he said, wagging his finger at me, "Don't you ever take off like that again! I've been worried sick about you. It was bad enough having Nestle missing; then you disappeared, too. The two of you will be lucky if I *ever* let you out again!" he yelled, as he emphasized the word "ever" and ushered us in the front door with his foot. What a shock to my sensitive system! Here I was, expecting a pat on the back for finding Nestle; and instead, getting a kick in the ass for being gone so long. Where was the justice?

66

That's what I get for being a "do gooder," a "community creature," I thought. "Life sure isn't fair," I groused. And while all this was running through my mind, I pictured BR's head nodding in the affirmative. I could almost hear him saying, "That's right, Nathan; life isn't fair -- so get over it!"

I seriously considered reverting to my former *modis operandi* -- doing things that made me feel good -- rather than doing things that made me feel good *about myself* -- until I looked at Nestle. As he nuzzled me, it was hard to ignore the adoration in his eyes or resist the love that radiated from his heart.

I could have easily over-reacted to The Won's unjustifiable anger and defended myself, but I stayed quiet instead. I was getting better at exercising restraint of pen and tongue, so to speak. I knew I hadn't really done anything wrong. And, given the same circumstances, I'd do exactly the same thing all over again. But I did understand his feelings. That didn't make him right, but I could be bigger than he was -- big enough to forgive his lapse of gratitude. (BR always said a sure-fire formula for serenity was starting every day by giving five others permission to be wrong without calling them on it. And today I decided that I'd rather be serene than right.)

Surprised by my own wisdom and graciousness, I wondered if I was getting old. Then I pulled out a grey whisker -- a sure sign I was getting old -- until I remembered, I was an *all grey* cat.

Chapter Eight

Sibling Rivalry -- The Other Side

ANGUS

Meow! Meow! Meee-owww! Pay attention to me! I am Angus and I have something to say! I'm as important as anyone else in this family!

Let me tell you the real story about how I fell down that chimney. It's true Nathan found me; but it was all his fault I was on the roof in the first place. He drove me into hiding -- I had to get away from him. He was always around, big as life, using up all the air in the room and watching me. So I got as far away from him as I could without leaving the yard. (I wasn't allowed to yet.) And that's when I took the header down the chimney.

Nathan isn't the easiest cat in the world to live with, you know. He has an opinion about everything and feels compelled to share it. As a matter of fact, his water dish is inscribed "Everyone's Entitled To An Opinion -- Mine." I should know, I gave it to him. I didn't like Nathan when The Won first brought me home. (Incidentally, I was the one who tried to scratch his eye out from inside the kitty carrier.) Talk about being full of yourself -- Nathan sure was. All he did for the first few months was tell us how great he was and try to push us around, mostly out of his chair and off tabletops.

Nestle and I were glad he spent so much time across the street at the Murphy's or hanging out in front of BR's cage. Personally, it was tough enough adjusting to a new environment without dealing with Nathan's condescending attitude. I knew he considered me just another pretty face, because he treated me like a blonde, even though I was more white than blonde. He didn't have a very high opinion of me; but how did he think I trained The Won to let me in and out so quickly? That should have given him a clue to my intelligence. But, what the heck, it was better to have him underestimate me and think I was a talkative little twit than think I was a threat. There were advantages to being low man on the totem pole. No one had unrealistic expectations of me -- actually they didn't have any expectations at all, so I didn't have many responsibilities. That was fine with me, because I didn't care about power or status. I just wanted to have fun!

Nathan was always pretty "street smart," and I did learn a lot from him in that respect. He was a quick thinker, but a slow learner. BR was the only one whose opinion he respected; otherwise, he never would have entertained a new idea. He just didn't relate well to others. I am much better at interpersonal relations than Nathan because I'm not nearly as wrapped around my own axle. That boy needs to lighten up!

As far as The Won is concerned, he loves to answer me when I talk. And I have to give him credit for mastering cat language phonetically even though he has trouble with idioms (and his accent stinks). But he tries, bless his heart. (I overheard Nathan comment that I can say anything I want about someone as long as I say, "Bless his heart" afterwards. It somehow takes the sting out of criticism). The Won loves to play with me, which I appreciate; but

69

I still straight-arm him when he picks me up. And I refuse to sit on his lap. It just isn't good for my image.

I never was very demonstrative because the cattery where I spent my formative months didn't encourage "feelings." No one ever expressed theirs, so I never learned to identify mine. Today I know that happiness is living with The Won, and I demonstrate mine by dancing around the house on my tiptoes, my tail tightly curled over my back like a squirrel. I assume The Won knows he has something to do with my happiness. Perhaps when I'm older, I'll tell him outright!

My brother, Nes, my favorite in the family, is the strong silent type and probably the most intelligent of the lot. Nes has no pretentions. He just slips away emotionally and physically when he feels like it and does his thing. I often wondered who he hung around with when he was out, but it soon became apparent that he's very democratic! He regularly visits *all* the humans on the block -- a real social butterfly. He seems to favor the human species over his own...except for me, of course.

I know Nes loves me, even though he is reserved. (He was raised in the same cattery of frozen feelings I was.) Today we sumo wrestle all the time, eat and sleep together, and even wash each other occasionally. I know I can count on Nes if I ever get in trouble; and he, of course, can always count on me because we're bro's. (I wish we could have matching black satin jackets for the three of us with "Clarke Cats" lettered on the back. Then everyone would know we are members of the same "gang" -- either that, or they'd think we were in a bowling league.)

70

I could say a lot more -- I often do -- but I guess I need to defer to Nestle.

NESTLE

I'm Nestle, a truly inappropriate name for a very sophisticated cat like myself; but what can you do when someone names you after the color of your chocolate ears -- someone who obviously has an eating disorder. Out of everyone in the family, I appear to be the most reserved. Nathan has his caretaker role to play, while Angus assumes the part of the clown. Being the middle cat, I don't feel I have anything to prove; thus I am pretty serene most of the time. I don't worry very often, but when I do, even that seems to work in my favor; because 90 percent of the things I worry about never happen.

My appointment with life is now and I try to live it to the fullest. I've always been an optimist so I tend to look on the positive side of life, finding reasons to say yes to requests rather than excuses to say no. Even in the most adverse situations, I try to find something for which to be thankful. In the case of the shrub incident, for example, I was thankful I was at least in the shade rather than being baked all day by the sun. I also try to be easy on myself when I do something foolish. And I did forgive myself for being careless and getting trapped, while being grateful that Nathan "saved" me. But even if he hadn't, I knew that someone else probably would have. That's faith. As long as I look for lessons in adverse situations, I don't have to keep repeating the same mistakes. My only regret about such incidents is that they cause my family such distress.

As far as my family is concerned, I am grateful to The Won for worrying about me and providing for me; so I'm as affectionate as he wants me to be. I love Nathan for being the control freak that he is, thinking he is responsible for Angus and I, even though he's not. So I treat him with respect while still going my own way. And I love Angus for just being Angus, a little scatterbrained loud-mouth with whom I play and give massive doses of attention. My relationship with Angus is best expressed by the phrase, "I love you not for who you are but who I am when I am with you." And what I am when Angus is around is a kinder, gentler and more compassionate version of myself.

I try not to be too self absorbed, but I am a Clarke, after all; and self-centeredness is a family trait. (The Won is so egocentric, for example, he thinks that when Nathan, Angus or I talk, we are talking to him. I guess it never occurs to him that we are talking to each other!) At any rate, I've talked too much and it's time to turn this back to Nathan.

Chapter Nine

The Enemy Among Us

They say everyone who was alive at the time JFK was assasinated remembers exactly where they were when they heard the traumatic news he'd been shot. Well, I feel the same about the day Dingo moved into the neighborhood, an equally traumatic event for me!

I was sitting at the top of the hill, as usual, master of all I surveyed, when the neighbors who lived at the bottom of our cul-de-sac drove up in their station wagon. I didn't have to actually see Dingo to know he was there. I heard him from the time the car entered the neighborhood, even though his barking was slightly muffled by the closed car windows. I didn't particularly like Dingo's family, so I was already predisposed to disliking Dingo as well. The family was pretty strange. The mother kept running away from home, hiding out in church basements for days; while the father rarely came home at all. And no one blamed either for avoiding their three obnoxious children whose principle activity was screaming at the tops of their lungs while beating on each other. As a group, they could have posed for *Psychology Today's* "Dysfunctional Family of the Year."

I guess the mother thought adding a dog to the family dynamics would bring them all closer together -- or at least divert the children's attention away from each other and her. But why she chose an animal that possessed no redeeming social values

73

whatsoever was a mystery to me and everyone else. To say this dog (part Australian Dingo) lacked the most rudimentary social skills was an understatement. It literally ran roughshod over the entire family and anything or anyone else that got in its way.

You might wonder what business this was of mine. The answer is plenty! Because from the moment Dingo arrived in the neighborhood, he made my life a living Hell. This dog was much stronger than any of the kids who walked him, so Dingo dragged them where *he* wanted to go. But that was academic since he rarely lasted more than five minutes on the leash. He regularly slipped his collar or broke free from their grip, the leash trailing behind him, as he spastically lurched around the neighborhood. It was only a matter of time before he'd spot me, Nes, or Angus outside, minding our own business, sunning in our yard. Then he'd race pell mell across the street, hell bent for leather up our hill, legs pumping and saliva flowing from his ugly jaws, intent on making dog food of us.

When he was after me, I felt like a deer caught in the headlights of an oncoming automobile, paralyzed by fear -- or like a passenger in a car at the end of a dark tunnel down which a speeding freight train is rushing. My heart would pound so hard I thought it would jump right out of my chest until the adrenalin kicked in, spurring me to run for my life -- and the patio door which The Won fortunately always left open for us. Imagine my shock when ol' Dingo chased me right through the door and into my own living room? I came "thisclose" to a very ugly end!

This dog was absolutely amoral. He had no sense of right and wrong. It's a good thing The Won was home to snatch me from the jaws of death and chase Dingo back outside; but I never felt exactly the same about the sanctity of my home again because Dingo had violated it. It's also a good thing Angus and Nestle were somewhere else at the time, because they would have been scared witless by the experience. I admit to being afraid and angry for my own safety; but nothing could vamp my righteous indignation like the thought of someone hurting either of them.

The Won was the most upset over Dingo's intrusion. And rightly so, since it was his primary purpose in life to keep us out of harm's way. Trying to control his anger, The Won promptly marched across the street to talk to Dingo's owners. I witnessed a lot of head-bobbing up and down on the part of the dog's master, but The Won didn't seem at all appeased by the conversation. My observation that his talk with our neighbor hadn't done much good was confirmed when, two days later, Dingo was once again on the loose, this time chasing Nestle through the patio door and into our living room.

After another trip across the street and another conversation with the family, The Won felt he had no recourse except to call Animal Control. But the way he slammed down the phone when he was finished talking to them suggested we'd find no relief forthcoming from that quarter either. It wasn't fair! We were here first! This was our neighborhood! Cats, because of our silent superiority and unintrusive nature are supposed to be able to roam freely; while dogs, because of their numerous neuroses, crude behavior, and hypersensitivity, are wisely required by law to be restrained at all times. Clearly the law should have handled this situation; but since it looked as though neither the law nor the owners were going to do anything to restrain Dingo, it was up to me to take matters into my own hands! I'd been nursing this resentment long enough and was tired of dealing with my chronic anger over it.

In all fairness to The Won, I should add here that he did the best he could to protect us. At great financial and personal expense, he constructed an elaborate network of iron fencing, bungee sticks, and barbed wire all along the perimeter of the yard. The railings were spaced just far enough apart to allow us in while keeping Dingo out. This system wasn't foolproof, but it certainly gave us the advantage when running to safety with Dingo in hot pursuit. Personally, I thought the problem of Dingo needed to be eliminated in its entirety.

As usual, I brought my case to BR for a second opinion. Although safe in his cage, he was nonetheless sympathetic. Greatly disturbed by the sudden shift in the neighborhood's balance of power, he counseled me that the only way to handle any unpleasant situation is to ACE it: Accept it; Change it; or Eliminate it. And where Dingo was concerned, we both favored the latter option. (If the CIA could "sanction" its political enemies, I could certainly dispose of mine, particularly one with such a rabid personality! Living in Washington made it easy to rationalize such political decisions.) Now all we had to do was select the method.

Although I spent a good part of my life seeing if I could run up and kiss the devil on the lips, I'd grown more cautious with age-- and more humble, too. Overcoming my pride and fear of rejection, I once again performed the ultimate act of humility by asking for help -- from the same Gang of Four who'd assisted me with the "cage" incident. There was strength in numbers. Besides, I liked them. They were optimists who saw the opportunities in every difficulty rather than the difficulties in every opportunity.

We put our heads (and five sets of pointed ears) together to devise a plan to remove Dingo, who was getting bolder by the day. His family didn't help matters by hanging what looked suspiciously like a cat tail from a tree in his yard, encouraging him to tear it apart for his amusement. I felt a little sad that we had to go to this extreme when Dingo's errant behavior might have been corrected under the guidance of a healthier family (or a stint in military school), but c'est la vie! And there was no time to waste since Nestle and Angus were both now being pursued by Dingo on a regular basis.

Recognizing that success results from a critical marriage between preparation and opportunity, our peculiar little task force went to work. First, we considered luring Dingo out in front of a speeding car, but felt that was too violent. Besides, whoever acted as bait could conceivably get run over as well. Then we thought about taking turns having him chase us around the tree to which he was tied, until he was so entangled in his lead, he'd choke himself to death. But, again, that seemed unnecessarily cruel. So we finally settled on the most diabolical plan of them all. Brilliant in its simplicity, the scheme only required our fastest sprinters and intelligence I'd already gathered, courtesy of The Won. I could have carried it out myself, just using Angus and Nestle; but I wanted to keep them safe, and there was an element of danger.

When The Won previously called Animal Control to complain that Dingo was running lose again, he'd been told there was little they could do about it. I overheard him complain to someone that, although Animal Control did patrol the area and pick up strays on Tuesdays, Dingo wasn't considered a stray as long as he stayed close to home. The Won was so frustrated and obsessed with the situation, he kept a pair of binoculars and a gun by the window. And as soon as he knew Dingo was off the leash, he'd frantically call us in, arming himself, ready to shoot Dingo should the dog have the audacity to follow us in our house again.

I gave The Won credit for mounting an intelligent and effective defense, but I could never picture him really shooting Dingo. He was too much of an animal lover. However, he'd never have to make that decision since he'd already provided me with all the information I needed to take care of Dingo for once and for all.

So the next Tuesday, when The Won started frantically calling us home, I knew Dingo had just slipped his collar for the last time. But instead of fleeing inside with Angus and Nestle like I normally did, I took off on a dead run *Kamikaze*-like, straight into Dingo's path. Myself and the Gang of Four then took turns leading Dingo astray, letting him chase us through bushes and over fences, luring him further and further away from the neighborhood. When we were sure he was totally disoriented and completely lost, we disappeared, leaving him to whimper and sniff around in circles-- until the Animal Control van came rumbling around the corner. At that opportune moment, I streaked in front of Dingo who, in turn, exposed himself to the officers in the van. They couldn't help noticing that Dingo was collarless and tagless, and the rest was history...

We watched with great glee as Dingo excitedly leapt at the moving vehicle before being captured and herded into its innermost recesses by the Animal Control officers. Tongue hanging out, head swiveling from side to side with a stupid expression on his face, Dingo looked eager to be "rescued." And we were equally eager to see him taken away. Dumb Dog!

We were sure that was the last we'd see of Dingo, but we were wrong. His family eventually found and "sprung him" from the pound. He was around to torment us for a few more months, during which I taught Angus and Nestle to be much more cautious when they were outdoors. BR said that a wise man learned from his mistakes; and, believe me, we had. However, BR also said that a wiser man learned from someone else's, an ideal towards which I promised myself I'd strive in the future.

Angus and Nestle were right that it wasn't fair they had to temper their freedom because of Dingo's illegal forays, but I had to break the news to them that life wasn't always fair. And by teaching them, I relearned the same lesson. Since I couldn't seem to eliminate or change the situation regarding Dingo, I had to learn to accept it and change my attitude. And, lo' and behold, time finally took care of the problem, as it often does. Dingo's entire family was finally taken away in a van --a moving van that transported them to a new town where they became someone else's problem.

There were other dogs in the neighborhood, of course, who'd never particularly bothered me or my brothers. I did notice, after Dingo left, however, that they gave us an even wider berth than usual. I even thought I detected a trace of new-found respect in their eyes when they looked at me as they passed -- safely on the end of their leashes. But maybe it was just my imagination.

Chapter Ten

More Lives Lost

I realized The Won and I were getting old when we started spending more time reminiscing about the past than talking about the present or planning for the future. It was clear my life had provided The Won with a lot of vicarious thrills -- at my expense, I might add. It was astounding how many times I came close to slipping over the edge, so to speak, as one life after another (of my alotted nine) circled the drain -- mostly when I was a naive kitten.

Life One was lost the time I was inadvertently locked in the neighbor's garage for days without food or water because I wasn't paying attention to what was happening around me. Life Two was spent hurtling down the inside of the chimney, the result of pursuing a bird with reckless abandon. And Life Three nearly expired for the same reason albeit when I was more mature.

I'd been watching a red-headed woodpecker hammer at the tall locust tree in the backyard each morning for days. At first I thought he was making that racket just to annoy me; but he was really after the bugs inside the rotting trunk. He didn't seem to care how much noise he made; and I was proud of my initial tolerance over his incessant banging -- until it gave me such a headache, I had to stop him.

Camouflaging my face with dirt and cobwebs like a commando, I stealthfully climbed up the trunk of the tree until I was parallel to him. After carefully testing my weight on a nearby branch, I lunged, attempting a clean snatch and jerk. Unfortunately, I missed the woodpecker completely, but managed to grab onto another smaller limb with my front paws. I was about to swing my back feet onto the limb when I heard a loud, ominous cracking sound.

I had just enough time to see the woodpecker fly away before I started falling like a stone to the ground, 100 feet below. A scene from an episode of "The Wild Kingdom" flashed through my mind; and, in that split second, I recalled how flying squirrels (like Rocky) flattened themselves out when airborne and gracefully glided to the ground. So I tried the same maneuver which, I am positive, saved my life. By the time I landed on the moss below, my fall was softened enough to merely knock the wind out of my sails rather than kill me.

After I dusted myself off, I looked around to make sure The Won was nowhere in sight. If he'd witnessed my accident he'd never let me outside again, I was sure -- or at least not for a very long time. But he hadn't. I learned some important lessons that day: never go out on a limb for anyone; and live and let live. The next time the woodpecker's hammering bothered me, I moved to a part of the yard where I couldn't hear it -- a novel concept.

I could claim no responsibility for losing Life Four...that rested entirely on the shoulders of the two little boys who lived across the street. (This family was nearly as peculiar as Dingo's. The mother always let the four- and five-year old boys play in their front yard nude. Personally, I found the human form *au naturalle* a little repulsive.) At any rate, on Halloween the boys were dressed --

81

a most unusual occurrance in itself-- as cowboys. Playing in their yard, waiting for their mother to take them trick or treating, they seemed harmless enough as I walked by on my way to BR's.

I was thinking about the latest affront visited upon me by life and rehersing how I'd present the information to BR to elicit his sympathy, so I wasn't as alert as I should have been. And before I knew what hit me, they did. They snatched me off my feet; and while one held me down, the other proceeded to tie me up with the lasso that accessorized his costume. Initially, I was just embarrassed that I'd let myself be captured by these two little monsters. But when the rope started tightening around my neck, literally choking me to death, my embarrassment turned to out-and-out fright. I kicked out with my back feet as hard as I could, claws extended to the max, while sinking my teeth into the soft flesh of an arm. They both squealed in unison, as much from surprise as real pain, and dropped me like a hot rock. Taking advantage of the confusion, I dashed away as fast as I could. I swore I'd never again trust anyone under 30, but the real lesson was the same one I kept learning over and over again -- to stay in the now, be mindful of my surroundings, and only talk to those who are present.

The loss of Life Five was entirely The Won's fault. It was winter and he'd decided he needed a vacation somewhere tropical to escape the sub-zero temperatures and ice storms we'd been experiencing for weeks. He'd arranged for a friend to housesit and take care of me the two weeks he'd be gone. I hated to see him leave -- it was like watching my electric blanket walk out the door. We spent a lot of quality time together in the house during the winter months; but I knew he'd go whether I approved or not. So, putting the best face on the situation, I tried to view it not as a problem, but as an opportunity -- an opportunity to train yet another adoring human to do my will.

I knew as soon as "friend" Jack walked in the front door, he wasn't a cat *aficionado*. The Won was falling all over himself introducing us, while Jack...whom I nailed as an irresponsible dandy -- totally ignored me in favor of checking out his new accommodations. Talk about misdirected priorities! I cocked my head at The Won, displaying my chagrin at Jack's lack of interest in me. But it was too late for The Won to change plans since he was due at the airport in an hour. Patting me on the head, The Won said a few words to Jack about how well he knew we'd get along, before reluctantly going out the door. Little did The Won or I suspect that I'd shortly follow.

As soon as Jack heard The Won's car go up the hill, he opened the patio door and invited me outside. I really didn't want to go...even though it was early afternoon, it was already freezing out there. But it seemed I had no choice in the matter. Jack picked me up under the arms and unceremoniously tossed me out and onto the deck.

I hugged the side of the house for about an hour, jogging in place to stay warm, before scratching at the glass patio door to be let in. I waited a few minutes for Jack to get the message and open it, but I could see his feet hanging over the arm of the couch in the living room and they weren't moving. I scratched some more, waited some more, then gave up for awhile, concluding the lazy s.o.b. was probably napping, all warm and cozy, while I froze my tail off.

83

Positioned with my nose to the patio door, I watched my breath fog the glass as I waited patiently for Jack's feet to hit the floor. My whiskers were laden with ice and I was mincing from the cold by the time they did. I'd also developed a major resentment about being virtually abandoned in the dead of winter. I'd give him a piece of my mind as soon as I got in the house, I thought, tail whipping from side to side as I readied myself to make a mad dash for the kitchen as soon as he opened the door. But he never did. The bastard looked right through me as he passed from the living room into the kitchen for a snack on which I hoped he'd choke.

I kept going back to my house every day, my nose pressed against the glass, my stomach rumbling from hunger, and my body chilled to the bone -- weakly pawing at the door, begging Jack to let me in. But Jack continued to ignore my pathetic presence. So, for two entire weeks, I was left to cadge food from garbage cans and try to keep warm as best I could by sleeping in the narrow crawlspace between the house and deck. I kept having flashbacks of the porch of my kittenhood, obsessing about coming full circle, feeling depressed and sorry for myself, and hating the earthy smell that once again permeated my coat. I couldn't believe this was really happening to me!

Then, on the fourteenth day, when I thought I couldn't take it any more, I heard the distinct and distant rumble of The Won's car descending the hill in front of the house. Tears of joy spilled down my frosty cheeks as I raced pell mell down the stairs to meet him, nearly bowling him over when I jumped into his arms.

"You feel a little light, Nathan," he said, hugging me to his chest. Then he held me at arms length for closer inspection, appalled by what he saw. I was dirty; I was cold; and I was thin, a condition I never suspected I'd experience, much less complain about. "It's apparent Jack has fallen down on the job," The Won said -- an understatement if I ever heard one.

I was so deliriously happy The Won was home, all I wanted to do was curl up on his chest in my warm house -- after I ate, that is. I hoped The Won would get even with Jack for the way he mistreated me; but right now it was impossible to be hateful when I was feeling so grateful. I never again took my food and shelter for granted. And I made sure The Won never again took another extended vacation...without me.

Life Six expired as a result of my early contact with Dingo; Life Seven, a close call at the hands (or mouth, I should say) of a mean mother opossum upon whom I accidentally stumbled while she was dumpster diving in our garbage. Ordinarily opossums didn't scare me, but this one was foaming at the mouth and had a glazed look in her eye, a sign she was either rabid or just plain crazy. Knowing the difference between courage and foolhardiness, I escaped being bitten by leaving rather hastily. Had I not already been taught a little humility, I probably wouldn't have had the good sense to "spit and run away, so I could live to spit another day."

When I recounted these experiences to BR, I ascribed escaping my "close calls" to luck. But BR insisted my death kept getting interrupted because my work wasn't done -- whatever that meant. His philosophy was a bit mystic for me.

I believed there was an inherent amount of danger just living life and getting older. And I accepted that some days were

85

going to be tougher than others. (BR used to say, "Some days you eat the bear; and some days the bear eats you.") But I also concluded, based on my experience, that city life was far more dangerous than survival in the wild. (It really was a jungle out there!) I couldn't very well relocate, however; because long ago I'd committed to being with The Won "till death do us part." And that meant, as long as he stayed in this neighborhood, so would I. Wasn't that what commitment was all about?

Chapter Eleven

Deja Vu All Over Again

I couldn't believe it was spring again. The years were just flying by. And typical of a Washington spring day, a steady drizzle fell from the slate grey sky onto budding flowerbeds that would burst forth into bloom as soon as the sun shone.

I despaired of Washington weather. In summer it was so hot and humid it felt as though a gigantic, steaming, woolen blanket had been thrown over the city; and in winter it was just cold and raw enough for the streets to be coated with an annoying sheet of ice or snow that soon turned to unattractive rust-colored slush. (Native Washingtonians, an endangered species, had no idea how to drive in ice or snow, but neither did anyone else it seemed. No matter where people originally hailed from --even Chicago and Buffalo -- their winter driving skills vanished as soon as they crossed the District line.) And, as if ice and snow didn't make winter unpleasant enough, the city was notorious for its legendary potholes, the size of bomb craters, which regularly swallowed cars and people whole.

For the most part, the fall and spring weather made living in Washington tolerable -- once you got past the spring days that were spoiled by a steady, driving rain, like today. I hated rain, but BR said it sounded like applause to him -- a time to catch his breath between performances. And, life, after all, was merely a series of performances. BR was a bit of a Pollyanna, I thought, and just full

87

of show biz analogies. He also kept reminding me to live life to the fullest, because today was real -- and not a dress rehersal!

My day hadn't started out on a high note, so I decided to drop in on BR, even though I didn't particularly like the way his cage smelled when it rained -- all musty from the wet straw. When I got there, I was shocked by his appearance. His ears drooped; his eyes were aflame as though he suffered from a bad case of conjunctivitus; and his fur visibly sagged from what appeared to be a significant weight loss. I asked him how he felt, but he dodged the question by turning the conversation around to me. He knew there was no one I loved talking about more than me, so this always proved an excellent diversionary tactic.

Actually I'm not being fair to myself. I wasn't that self-centered anymore. My conversations with BR were often peppered with anecdotes about Angus and Nestle. Angus was as much of a chatterbox in adulthood as he'd been as a kitten. I'd never seen anyone so highly skilled in the art of making small talk. Even The Won, who initially thought this cute (sure it was only a "stage" Angus was going through), was getting tired of being followed around the house to the accompaniment of a steady stream of babble. The Won couldn't even escape outside, because Angus just followed him there, never skipping a beat in his soliloquies.

Nestle, on the other hand, was still the strong, silent type. But, then again, he was rarely around to say much. As soon as dusk settled over the neighborhood, Nestle was off and running -- a real night owl! Because he never returned home before dawn, The Won fantasized that Nestle led a fabulously exciting life. The truth was that Nestle did sleep around a lot -- but always alone.

In comparison, I was a model citizen. I stayed pretty close to home these days, only crossing the street when I went to visit BR. I was content sitting on top of the hill in front of the house watching Nestle descend into the sewer after a racoon; lie in wait next door for hungry birds; or sprawl in the middle of the street playing "chicken" with oncoming traffic. At my age, it was advisable to take vicarious pleasure in Nestle's antics rather than join him in them. I'd developed a basic "live and let live" attitude where the boys were concerned, but it hadn't always been that way.

When they entered early adolescence, I devoted nearly every waking hour to teaching them all the survival skills I thought they needed to know. Was there anyone else better suited to do this? And although they never thanked me directly for my time and effort, I knew they were grateful. How could they not be? I told myself I didn't need their thanks; my thanks was watching them put these skills into practice. But a little recognition would have been nice. It was over such a situation that I now sought BR's counsel.

Looking him straight in the eye, as he'd taught me to do, I told him what had happened. As I'd been about to begin another series of lectures on the "natural enemies" section of my Outdoor Survival Course, I'd become ill -- probably from something I ate in the yard. I knew Angus and Nestle would be disappointed by the postponement of their lesson, but what could I do? When I called them into the living room to tell them; however, The Won showed up instead.

Seating himself beside me, he patted my head, grateful, I was sure, for the initiative I was taking tutoring the boys. I felt perfectly justified complaining to him about their constant tardiness; but before I even got started, he stoppped me mid-sentence. He had something more serious to discuss, and I naturally assumed he wanted me to shoulder even more responsibility in the household. Although I felt over-extended as it was, how could I refuse? (I graduated *cum laude* from the School of Martyrdom.)

As diplomatically as he could, The Won confided that the boys were complaining that I was monopolizing too much of their time with my lengthy and laborious "life lectures." I flushed with embarrassment and indignation before opening my mouth to protest. But The Won wasn't finished. He said they felt like I had them in a choke hold, an iron paw pressed across their necks, as I force fed them what *I* thought they needed to know. The Won said they wanted to experience life for themselves, not vicariously through me recounting my experiences. And he said I should let them.

I was incredulous, then hurt, and finally angry at the ungrateful little bastards. The very idea they'd go behind my back and over my head to The Won and embarrass me this way! The thought made my stomach churn. I really wanted to get even with them for their betrayal, thinking of all the ways I could. But I settled for a medium-sized resentment instead, and a fervent wish they'd fall flat on their fuzzy faces the first time they encountered a problem they didn't know how to solve.

BR listened patiently, then said, "Nathan, if you insist on getting even, make it with someone who's been kind to you." He chuckled at his own cleverness, then calmly outlined the way he was sure this would all work out. Angus and Nestle would learn the necessary survival skills on their own -- not as perfectly as if I'd taught them, but well enough to get by. And, since I wouldn't be tied up tutoring them, I'd have all the time in the world to smell the roses (in the yard); take a census of the mole population; keep the squirrels in check; and do all the things I really wanted, but never had the time, to do. And Angus and Nestle *would* eventually come to me for advice when they needed it, proving I was as indispensible as I thought I was.

BR told me to stop trying to control them and accept them as they were. If I did, I'd finally be able to voluntarily let go of situations before I inevitably lost my grip on them anyway. BR assured me that this new attitude would guarantee me a much longer and more serene life. He said I was ready for this stage of maturity. It had been a long time coming; but that was natural. Meaningful self improvement for the long term was seldom accomplished in the short term. I felt better already.

After talking about Angus and Nestle, BR got a far off look in his eyes. I could tell he was getting ready to wax nostalgic about his family, and I was right. "Most everyone knows about my cousin, Bre're Rabbit," BR began, "But few have heard about the rest of my family -- Mere, my mother; Pere, my father, from whom I learned everything I know about life; and, Frere, my brother. Our last name was Lapin. We were French, you see. It was my brother and I who Americanized our last name to Rabbit after Mere and Pere died."

I never pictured BR part of a normal family, and I listened in fascination as he spun tale after tale about life in the rabbit hutch. When he talked about Pere's tragic death, I thought I saw a tear in his eye. He told me he was very young when his father was taken from him prematurely -- the direct result of a pregnancy test. BR related the anger and bitterness he'd felt over his father's murder at the hands of a mad scientist.

BR explained that, up until then, he'd believed in a benevolent power that ruled the universe. It was his mother who taught him about a kind and loving "Maker" who bestowed gifts on those who were good. When he was older Mere also told him the flip side of this arrangement, i.e. that this same "Maker" or God punished those who were bad -- or harbored bad thoughts, an offense of equal severity. (BR said he immediately threw out the source of all his bad thoughts -- his *Playboy* magazines with their centerfolds of bare bunnies -- because once he understood "the rules," he wanted to play by them).

From then on, BR was a pillar of virtue, living by The Golden Rule and doing everything he should in order to reap his just reward. So when Mere and Pere both died within months of eachother, he couldn't reconcile why such bad things were happening to such a good bunny as himself. Events did not conform to his concept of a loving Higher Power who always rewarded those who were good -- like Santa Claus. Instead, his God had acted like The Terminator, punishing him for no reason. He was so angry at this injustice, he turned his back on everything in which he'd ever believed and became a self-styled atheist. Objectively speaking, his life wasn't that bad. He ended up being raised and nurtured by a loving uncle who tried to assure him that sometimes bad things just happened to good people. But BR remained a bitter bunny! And his new total self reliance left him far from happy. There was a deep hole in his heart. Something important was missing from his life. But he was too angry and proud to admit that.

Years went by during which BR felt empty. He wanted desperately to feel loved and protected again -- to believe in something greater than himself -- a benevolent entity, like the Easter Bunny who generously bestowed brightly colored eggs on everyone. But he couldn't get past blaming his Higher Power for the cruelty of his parents' premature deaths. Then, when he was miserable enough, he allowed a mentor, who was much wiser than he, to teach him differently. The pupil was ready, so the teacher appeared.

BR's mentor and spiritual advisor explained that BR's confusion stemmed from his old perception of a Higher Power as a judge who rewarded or punished individuals based on their conduct. A loving Higher Power, he suggested, loved everyone, not because they were good, but because He was good. And BR's Higher Power had never abandoned him; he'd actually carried him through the difficult times and provided for his survival. The proof was that BR was alive and well today.

BR was encouraged to create his own image of a user-friendly Higher Power. He was told to think of this Higher Power as the spirit of the one who loved him the most. The visual image that came to mind was Bugs Bunny, because the uncle who'd raised him coincidentally looked like Bugs, had a sense of humor like Bugs, and only wanted what was best for BR -- BR's new criteria for a kinder, gentler Higher Power. And most important, Bugs wasn't perfect, so BR wouldn't have to be either.

93

But it wasn't enough to believe in a loving Higher Power, BR also had to learn to trust that Higher Power. If you looked at life as a vegetable garden, his mentor explained, it was your responsibility to plant the seeds and water the garden; but it was your Higher Power who decided when and what eventually grew. BR understood that it was his job to continue doing the "next right thing" to take care of himself -- practically, physically, mentally, emotionally and spiritually. And his Higher Power would take care of the the big picture, i.e. the way his life unfolded.

It was clear from BR's demeanor that he was at peace. Not only did he trust Bugs with his life; he also trusted Him with his death. I didn't want to hear about that, but BR insisted. He said he wasn't afraid of dying because it was just an opportunity to be with Bugs. "Besides," he said, "Life is fatal; and that's a fact!" BR further confided that he used to think if he were good, he'd be rewarded with a grand life in the hereafter. But he'd since learned that being good entitled him to that grand life right now -- right here on earth -- he didn't have to wait for the hereafter.

I listened politely to BR's views of a Higher Power; and even identified with the early tragedy of his parents' deaths. And considering his health, I was truly glad he wasn't afraid of dying. But personally, I thought he was a little naive. The only power in which I believed was my own -- and maybe The Won's -- but that was based exclusively on his ability to provide my food and shelter. I wasn't exactly a heathen; I just didn't happen to need a power greater than myself at this particular moment in time.

During the next week, I thought about visiting BR again, but I was in a bad mood and afraid he'd continue proselytizing

94

about a Higher Power. I'd heard enough for awhile; so I stayed away. But by the following week, my conscience bothered me sufficiently to propel me across the street -- even though I still didn't want to go.

When I got to the end of the driveway, I didn't see BR's cage. For a moment, my heart caught in my throat. I felt incredibly guilty I'd been so selfish. I visited BR when I was troubled and needy; but where was I when *he* needed *me?* I had better things to do, I answered myself sarcastically, while making a mental note to take the ass-kicking machine out of storage. Filled with trepidation, I hoped against hope that I'd find BR's cage in the garage, where I looked next. But I didn't.

"Oh my God, it's *deja vu* all over again!" I mentally screamed, parroting Yogi Berra. That hollow, sinking feeling I suffered when my family disappeared overcame me once more. I was being abandoned all over again -- and slipped into the same black hole of extraordinary sadness. But this time instead of burying my feelings, I allowed them to perculate to the surface in the form of tears. I'd learned the hard way that when you bury feelings, you bury them alive -- permitting them to survive and grow. So I took mine to The Won, who didn't understand why I suddenly found the inside of the house so attractive; but he was delighted to have me seemingly attached to his hip for awhile -- providing me with the unconditional love I so desperately needed.

I felt lost without BR, just as I'd felt lost after the disappearance of my family. I always thought isolating in order to "find myself" was the answer to pain, until BR taught me differently. He was the one who said, "Nathan, we don't 'find' ourselves; we 'create' ourselves -- by reaching out to others and being the best we can be. I thought about the last time I talked to BR. Remembering how at peace he was with his Higher Power lifted the heaviness from my heart.

I realized there was a big difference in the way I reacted to the disappearance of BR and the disappearance of my family. I'd changed. This time I was grieving for BR, the life he relished, and the loss of him in my life. I wasn't mired in self pity, using his death as an excuse to revisit every tragedy that had ever befallen me. And I was patient with myself. I knew grief wasn't an event; it was a process -- during which I'd suddenly feel incredible sadness, time and again, often when I least expected it. I also knew I had to experience grief my own way. There was no text book formula. And talking to others, like The Won, Angus, Nestle, and an assortment of friends and acquaintances -- when I was ready -- helped. I was no longer The Lone Ranger, dodging feelings like bullets. I was Tonto, with a lot of "*kimosabies*" whom I truly loved and trusted with the tender shoots of my feelings.

I now thought I understood the difference between spirituality and religion, which BR had been trying to teach me. Religion consisted of rules and rituals of someone else's making to honor God; while spirituality was our own expression of love for God which has only one rule --The Golden Rule -- whose practice results in kindness towards others and a feeling of wholeness within ourselves. BR was the most spiritual creature I'd ever known and I smiled when I remembered what else he said about being spiritual. He said, "When we achieve true spirituality, everything else is insignificant -- unfortunately, we have to deal with the insignificant anyway."

96

When I could finally go outside again without being drawn across the street like a magnet to the former site of BR's cage, I talked to some of the neighbors about him. This helped fill the hole his absence left in my heart. I'd been so self-absorbed, I thought I was his only *true* friend; but it turned out he befriended everyone in the neighborhood and they all visited him with some regularity. I also discovered that the others knew a heck of a lot more about BR than I did; because they asked him about his life rather than always talking about their own -- unlike me. I dominated our conversations with my petty problems and now felt ashamed -- but in that shame was lost my last vestige of arrogance.

What I found out about BR was rather shocking! It was no mistake he lived in that cage. BR was actually under house arrest for indiscriminate breeding. It seems he was a two-time loser -- he'd been caught impregnating hundreds of bunnies himself, plus master-minding a ring of young hares whom he taught to procreate more efficiently. He'd coach an over-anxious hare, who wanted to race pell mell down the hill and jump a female rabbit in the warren, to walk slowly down the hill instead -- and jump *all* the female rabbits in the warren.

It tickled me to picture BR an outlaw. How many years ago that must have been! He'd been incarcerated for as long as I'd known him -- no wonder he was so adamant about living one day at a time -- and no wonder he did it with such grace.

When I missed BR so much I thought I couldn't stand it, I'd visit his grave in the pet cemetary. When I looked at his head-stone, I marvelled at how much life he'd packed into that dash between the dates of his birth and death. I knew he was where he belonged -- with Bugs -- his spirit free to roam that big cabbage patch in the sky. But I still felt sad and cried until my eyes were as red as his used to be. But that was OK. I could hear him telling me, "Nathan, you're exactly where you're supposed to be, feeling exactly what you're supposed to be feeling."

He'd played such an important part in my life. It was ironic I'd started visiting BR because I felt sorry for him. I was sure his life wasn't very interesting and my visits would add immeasurably to its quality. Instead, he'd given me the greatest gift of all -- he'd converted the walls of my mind from mirrors to windows. And his life was more interesting than anyone I'd ever known -- even though it was lived mostly between his ears. I sincerely hoped I'd brought just a little bit of joy into his life; because he'd certainly brought a lot of enlightenment into mine.

Another quote came to mind when I thought of BR. "Life's highest achievement is surviving with dignity and courage a difficult fate...then teaching others how to do the same." BR'd certainly survived all the tragedies that had befallen him with dignity and courage, then taught me how to do the same.

Chapter Twelve

I See The Light

A residual effect of BR's death was my irrational fear that something terrible was going to happen to Angus, Nestle, The Won, or possibly all three. I was waiting for the other shoe to drop and now understood The Won's similar anxieties which fueled his neurotic over-protection of us. When his unfounded fear kicked in, we were usually confined to quarters for no apparent reason. So we obviously preferred to see The Won brimming with confidence in order to be able to come and go as we pleased.

At any rate, I was a chip off the old neurotic block when it came to suffocating those I loved when I was fearful. And at the present time, The Won was the target of my attention. My focus was on his health, and more particularly, his weight. I became obsessed, monitoring everything he ate. I also had good reason to be concerned about his nutrition. Because, although he said he believed in a balanced diet and carefully selected his daily menu from different major food groups, three of those food groups were fat, salt, and sugar. When he did eventually buy something that could be considered "health food," it normally evolved into a science project in the refrigerator, growing green mold until its origin was indistinguishable.

When The Won ate too much and gained weight, I visualized his arteries clogging with globules of fat, causing imminent death from heart failure. When he ate too little and lost weight, I was certain he was wasting away from a debilitating disease of unknown origin. There was no happy medium. But that wasn't new. Every fiber of my being eluded moderation.

And if I wasn't obsessing about The Won, it was only because my focus had shifted to Angus or Nestle. Angus was still a love child in the true sense of the word, avoiding any kind of conflict. Even when he hunted moles in the backyard, the only danger to them was being licked to death. Nestle used to joke that Angus' prey "takes a licking, but keeps on ticking." I knew Angus wasn't in danger from predators, but that wasn't necessarily the case with his prey. I was sure he'd contract some fatal disease from their germs.

My fears concerning Nestle stemmed from his aggressive behavior. He engaged in paw-to-paw combat almost every time he went outside. He'd regularly come home with tufts of fur hanging from his coat, the result of an enemy claw "combing." I suggested BR's philosophy of giving five others permission to be wrong each day without calling them on it; but Nestle never let reason influence his testosterone level. He had to be right -- and would fight to prove it. This, of course, ran counter to BR's "I'd rather be happy than right" approach to life.

Neither Angus nor Nestle appreciated my caretaking, particularly when it involved shadowing them around the neighborhood. They were actually embarrassed, but I didn't care what they or others -- who teased me mercilessly with their loud cat-calls -- thought. I just went about my business unconcerned about my image.

Not everyone made fun of my possessive behavior, however. Some of the female cats interpreted my devotion to my siblings as a sign of responsibility and maturity. I could have exaggerated my importance in Angus and Nestle's lives to make myself even more admirable in their eyes, but I didn't. Self promotion was no longer necessary because I'd finally developed some self-esteem.

Angus and Nestle often teamed up against me to escape my surveillance, which was frustrating. It was at such times that I needed to remember I had the ability to start my day over whenever I wanted. In other words, I could ultimately choose to have whatever kind of day I wished. And I knew it was as impossible to have a good day with a bad attitude as it was to have a bad day with a good attitude.

When I became frustrated and resentful at Angus and Nestle, it was usually beause I'd spent too much time thinking. If I thought about myself long enough, feeling bad was inevitable. The antidote was to do something physical. "Move a muscle, change a thought" worked for me; so I'd run around the yard until I felt better.

I wished The Won would follow my example and get more exercise. I thought him much too sedentary and encouraged him to jog by running away from him whenever he came outside to fetch me. I'd witnessed plenty of other out-of-shape humans in the neighborhood trading their dignity for health, running up and down the street no matter how ridiculous they looked. And I wished The Won would start doing the same. But he didn't seem to get the idea. He was always in one of two places -- his chair channel

101

surfing, or out in the yard planting yet more grass. (In his attempt to cover a few bare spots on the lawn, he'd used enough grass seed to plant RFK Stadium several times over; but the only thing that got greener was the inside of the nursery's cash register.)

It was ironic that I'd actually become a substitute for Angus, who'd followed The Won indoors and out as a kitten. In those days when The Won stopped short, he'd be wearing Angus. But my case was different because The Won and I were equals. We were very compatible, and becoming more alike with each passing day.

The Won and I were so close, we could almost read each other's minds, although we didn't have to rely on this method of communicating. As I previously mentioned, The Won was pretty good at phonetically mimicking my language; while I, who couldn't claim to be truly bilingual, was very proficient at English comprehension. Long gone were the days when The Won's rhetoric sounded like "bla, bla, bla, Nathan." Now I understood almost everything he said, although I do admit to selective hearing on occasion. As a matter of fact, I usually tuned out or went out when The Won began philosophizing after a few drinks -- effectively trading the hot air inside for the fresh air outside.

I thought about the months I spent hanging out across the street at Mrs. Murphy's when The Won first brought the boys home. My false pride and wounded feelings almost caused me to turn my back on The Won and my home. How different my destiny would have been if I'd chosen to remain with Mrs. Murphy in her small house. And that had nothing to do with materialism. BR made me understand that it wasn't the number of souveniers you

102

collected in life that counted, but rather the number of souls you touched -- and more souls were available to me here than at Mrs. Murphy's. BR also said that destiny wasn't as much a matter of chance as of choice. And I was glad I chose to stay with The Won.

There was no doubt in my mind that I was The Won's favorite. And, in retrospect, I guess I always had been. Angus required proportionately more attention from The Won when he was young; so it just seemed like he was the favorite for awhile. Now that Angus and Nestle spent most of their time outside, however; The Won and I had quality time to bond and explore much more mature themes of conversation (which always seemed health related).

I'd developed a stiffness in my hind quarters that caused me to limp occasionally, which The Won finally noticed. (He was usually too preoccupied with his own hypochondria to worry about mine.) Since he suffered similar discomfort, his sympathy prompted a quick trip to the vet who diagnosed yet another thing The Won and I had in common -- arthritis.

Although The Won took medication for his condition, I relied on a far superior home remedy for mine, one that worked best in summer. I'd wait until mid-afternoon, when the blazing Washington sun had baked the black asphalt of our driveway, then stretch out behind the car, letting the heat penetrate my aching bones and joints. A couple of hours a day of this treatment did wonders for my condition.

The Won suffered from a second health problem that I, fortunately, did not share. I diagnosed it as either early Alzheimers

103

or extreme absentmindedness. In either case, the symptoms were similar -- frequent careening around from room to room in rage and frustration trying to find things he'd just put down. Pencils, glasses, scissors, pills, and tools were often the objects of his search, until he started misplacing larger items -- like us.

He'd be calling Angus, for example, hollering out the back door, then hollering out the front door, then yelling up the living room stairs -- while Angus was standing next to him all the time. I knew The Won's absentmindedness was serious, but I didn't think it was life threatening. Boy was I wrong!

I remember the day well. It was a hot, sticky, typical August afternoon. My arthritic hips were killing me. I'd left the air-conditioning of the house for my personal sauna on the driveway and was curled up napping when I heard the front door slam. Opening one eye, I watched The Won climb into the front seat of our convertible parked in front of me. He was always forgetting to put the top up and afternoon thunderstorms this time of year were a fact of life.

When I heard the engine rev up, I stretched out waiting for the whir of the motor that raised the top. I must have fallen asleep instantly because the next thing I felt was a crushing pain in my midsection, like I was bearing the weight of the world. I didn't want to open my eyes for fear of confirming what I suspected was true. The weight I felt was our car backing over me.

From my flattened position on the driveway, I watched for The Won's feet to hit the ground running as soon as he realized what he'd done. But instead of turning off the engine and investigating the "bump" he'd run over, he put the car in forward and ran over me a second time. I couldn't believe it! I must have been in shock -- from his sheer stupidity, if nothing else -- because I didn't feel anything the second time the car rolled over me.

"Oh my God, what have I done?" The Won cried in horror as he realized the "bump" in the driveway was me. He bolted from the car, ran around behind it, and found me lying in the driveway looking like a fur rug.

I don't remember too much after that because I drifted in and out of consciousness -- in the car racing to the vet, stretched out on the stainless steel operating table, then finally home again. When I fully came to, I felt a throbbing in my hind legs which were bandaged with some sort of splint locking them in place. I hurt; but I didn't hurt as much as I thought I should, so I must have been given some mind-altering substance.

I vaguely recall the vet's amazement at my physical condition when he first saw me. By all rights, I should have been dead. But the weight of the car had forced all of my internal organs up into my chest, underneath my rib cage, which conveniently expanded to accommodate them. I looked remarkably like Superman -- minus his blue jersey with the big red "S" and a matching pair of tights.

Although the vet had never seen anything like my condition before, his educated guess was that the force of gravity would redistribute my internal organs to where they were supposed to be, without his help. And he was right. It happened just that way. Unbelievably, the only real damage had been to my ego and back hips, which mended in record time with the help of the splint. And I was soon normal again, my physical being unchanged. But I couldn't say the same for my perception of life.

By all rights, I should have died on August 24 -- the day The Won ran over me. And I wondered why I hadn't. Why had my death been interrupted? Was there a greater purpose to my life? Was something else controlling it? I remembered feeling so at peace when I was slipping in and out of consciousness, all of my worldly concerns removed. I saw that brilliant white light others teetering on the edge of death have described, and I was overcome with an incredible sense of well-being. I intuitively understood I was no longer in control of my life. It was as though...yes...I'd lost my power...and it had been replaced by a higher one, a Higher Power. Could it be ? I'd turned my life over to a Higher Power and felt real peace and serenity for the first time in my life? Was this what BR had been talking about?

But try as I might, I just couldn't imagine Bugs Bunny as this Higher Power. The picture was all wrong. Bugs may have been a fine concept for BR; but it did nothing for me. I needed to create my own image, one that was both Nathan-friendly and species-friendly. I was relieved to have finally arrived at this spiritual place. BR had warned me, tongue-in-cheek, that many who count on "being saved" at the eleventh hour die at 10:30.

I found it comforting to believe in a Higher Power that I trusted implicitly with the rest of my life. Gone was the confusing celestial entity that gave with one hand and took away with the other. I'd experienced first-hand the presence and unconditional love of this new Higher Power who'd put BR in my life and who'd also given me a second chance to live it to the fullest. The simple prayer, "I sought my soul which I could not see; I sought my God, who eluded me. Then I sought a friend, and I found all three," epitomized my experience.

I knew BR, wherever he was, would be smiling from above when I chose to call the gentle, supernatural force that would guide the rest of my life my "Higher Meower." It would take time to attach a visual image to this Higher Meower. Would it be Garfield? Sylvester? Morris? But I had plenty of time. (My thoughts again drifted to BR. He used to say that time takes time; that the concept of time is necessary to keep everything from happening at once.)

I learned so much from BR. I also remembered his analogy of life being a boat ride with him doing the rowing and his Higher Power doing the steering. BR said it was always a smooth voyage unless he insisted on taking over the steering. His "God" would always let him steer, if he really wanted to, but the boat never went anywhere -- because "God don't row; it's not in His contract." And speaking of contracts, I decided to symbolically sign one of my own with my Higher Meower for the management of my life. And I'd do it at the pet cemetary, standing in front of BR's grave. It seemed only fitting.

I'd always idolized The Won, but causing my accident did knock him off the pedestal on which I'd placed him. I wasn't angry with him though -- because he felt so badly about it, and because I'd found my Higher Meower as a result of it. When I was a kitten and The Won disappointed me, he'd say he was only human. I now understood just how much of an admission of inferiority that was.

Another gift of finding my Higher Meower was recognizing that The Won, Angus, and Nestle also had their own, and I no longer had to feel responsible for them. I also stopped praying for what *I* wanted them to have. I finally realized I didn't know what their happiness, serenity, or well-being looked like to them. I had to live my own life, just doing the next right thing and letting my Higher Meower take care of everything else. And I would do my best to practice being spiritual (a matter of wholeness rather than holiness).

I was finally at peace with who Nathan was -- neither passive nor aggressive, defensive nor offensive, choosing my behavior rather than reacting to someone else's. I'd gone from Nathan, King of Beasts, when I was a precocious "only" cat protecting my turf, to Father Nathan, akin to Mother Theresa, benevolent guardian of those poor unfortunates put in my charge (i.e., Angus and Nestle), to just plain old Nathan, accepting who I am today while ever striving to be better. I've made a successful transition from a *do-be* (having to *do* something in order to *be* someone) to a more humble *I-am*. And today *I am somebody*, just like I always wanted to be.

Chapter Thirteen

Nathan, New and Improved

I'm pleased I have another lease on life, but this is my last. I've used up eight lives so far and I'm nearing number nine. Almost seventeen years have passed since The Won brought me home, so I must accept the reality that my time is running out. BR used to say that happiness is knowing your limitations, and I am fully aware of mine.

The Won is no spring chicken either, I keep reminding myself. It used to tear me up when I noticed him getting slower, greyer, and more forgetful -- because I didn't want to be reminded I, too, was getting slower, greyer, and more forgetful. However, once I adjusted to my own aging gracefully, I also adjusted to his. And today I take comfort in the fact we are growing old together.

It's a shame youth is wasted on the young. (Who said that?) It has taken me so long to appreciate life, there isn't much of it left to appreciate. And now that I know how to live it to the fullest, I don't have the necessary energy. But, for the most part, I am content living life as it is, not as I wish it to be. And I honestly feel I am leading a life well led.

Many of life's mysteries have been solved with time, including he disappearance of Runaway Sue. I'd always felt I was so insignificant in her life that she'd just chosen to leave me and make a new life for herself. (That kind of reasoning should have been a clue to my low self esteem, but no one talked of such things then.) I, of course, realized she wasn't like other momcats, but I never judged her. I was actually proud she dared to be different. As far as parenting is concerned, today I realize that "if she'd have known better, she would have done better." I was so resigned to the idea that she left me voluntarily, I was shocked to accidentally learn she hadn't abandoned me, after all. She'd been tragically killed by a car that same morning she left the porch, never to return. Her mind must have been on the disappearance of the litter when she wandered into the street and in the path of an on-coming car.

I thought I'd come to terms with her death a long time ago, but I was only fooling myself. I'd processed her disappearance intellectually, but not emotionally. The way I dealt with it was by not dealing with it. And now that I accepted what her loss really meant to me, I could finally grieve and be at peace.

As for my "wombmates," I learned through the same source that they indeed had been taken away and adopted. And two of them actually lived less than a mile from me -- small world! I haven't as yet taken the time to look them up; but I will, because "family" is becoming more important to me the older I get. (And, besides, taking the initiative to meet them in the near future could prevent the embarrassment of being reunited with them on an upcoming Oprah show!)

I now realize that Runaway and my siblings always had their own Higher Meower -- One that looked after them just as mine has always looked after me -- because we are all God's creatures. Indeed, I realize that the highest position I can attain in life is that to which I was born, i.e. creature of God. So, what was I trying to prove all those years? Why did I feel I had to prove myself worthy? According to BR, I was born worthy. And all of the events in my life that I considered so important at the time pale in comparison to my relationship with my Higher Meower and those within and outside of my species. And that's the most important lesson I've learned.

My attitude about everything seems to have come full circle over the years. I no longer want to be in control of the outcome of my efforts, because I firmly believe that God bestows the greatest gifts on those who let him choose (the outcome). And I no longer want to feel responsible for anyone else's life or happiness. What a relief! As soon as I stopped taking myself so seriously and realized there were no "big deals" (unless I could die from them), I began to enjoy life.

On a practical level, I've delegated the protection of the Clarke turf to Angus and Nestle, and wonder why I didn't do that a long time ago. I've finally let go without leaving claw marks on everything. I find I'm happy most of the time -- another revelation! And my happiness isn't dependent on external things or circumstances anymore. Like BR said, it's an inside job. It comes about by improving my relationships with my Maker and everyone around me.

BR also used to tell me I had to love myself before I could learn to love others. And today I've accomplished both. When I was young and cocky, I didn't care enough about anyone else to empathize with their problems, much less sympathize with their feelings. But today I feel real compassion for everyone and

111

everything -- crying at poignant moments; crying on sad occasions; crying on happy occasions; crying at weddings, funerals, and when Lassie Comes Home. What a pleasure it is to feel, even though not all of my feelings are always good ones. But it doesn't matter, because the bad ones don't last very long these days and the good ones last much longer than ever before.

One of the keys to good living is being the best Nathan I can be. I have to work at it every day because as soon as I start to coast, I'm headed down hill. I recognize that I am only responsible for the effort, not the outcome. Many things in my life have changed, because that's what life is about -- change. BR used to say "change is certain, but growth is optional."

I've learned I can't control the wind; but I can re-adjust my sails. And if I do the best I can today, I won't have to spend tomorrow regretting yesterday. I remember when my most fervent wish was for a cat door, a double dish, a new feather-on-a-stick. I once asked for all things so I could enjoy life; and instead I was given life so I could enjoy all things. And I do enjoy everything today -- from sharing moments, a meal, and intelligent conversation with The Won to long periods of quiet solitude, appreciating everything I've ever been given.

My perspective on life today is certainly far different from what it was before I met BR. As a matter of fact I like to think of my life in terms of BR (Before Rabbit) and AR (After Rabbit) because he changed it so markedly. He led me from an existence of "dancing as fast as I can" to one of serenely waltzing through life.

BR's legacy to me was all of his wisdom. He used to tell me, "Nathan, life is not a problem to be solved, but rather a journey to be enjoyed." If you absolutely insist on enjoying life, I can suggest some basic rules to live by -- rules to insure a serene life:

1. Recognize you have no control over other people, places or things.

2. Believe that your life and everyone else's rests in the hands of a loving Higher Power.

3. Have faith that Higher Power has the *best* long range plan in mind for you -- a plan far beyond your limited imagination.

4. Find out who you are by evaluating your strengths and weaknesses rather than judging yourself or others.

5. Talk to someone you admire and trust about that evaluation to get an objective opinion.

6. Be willing to change for the better.

7. Ask for help in doing just that.

8. Keep your side of the street clean with respect to your treatment of others.

9. Make amends when necessary. And "amends" means changing your behavior; not merely apologizing for it.

10. Take your emotional temperature daily so you can stop

negative thoughts and behavior before they reach a fever pitch.

11. Talk to your Higher Power frequently and listen to Him respond through the mouths of others and through your own insight and intuition.

12. Practice these principles on a daily basis and teach them to others.

When I listened to BR, I was always fidgeting with my feather-on-a-stick, which he, of course, noticed. He knew I had a very short attention span and an even shorter memory, so he summarized his suggestions into single-word goals: Honesty; Hope; Faith; Integrity; Trust; Willingness; Humility; Love; Justice; Perseverence; Spirituality; and Generosity.

Looking back on my life, I now realize that my Higher Meower always fulfilled my needs and never gave me more than I could handle. I have years of proven experience that He's always known what was best, so who am I to ever question His plans for me? Today I am confident that no matter what I ask of Him, He only has one of three answers for me: yes, later, or I have something better planned for you. And if it's I have something better planned for you, I have the patience and faith to wait to see what that is.

No longer do I find it necessary to bat birds, stampede squirrels or intimidate butterflies. Today I try to neither set conditions, have expectations nor make judgments regarding other creatures within and outside of my species. Today I am at peace with myself and in harmony with others. And as long as I remember I am powerless over other people, places, and things, and that the only thing I can really change is my attitude, my life is serene.

BR taught me that the key to being happy, joyous and free is getting out of myself by helping others (which I try to do with Angus and Nestle -- when I can catch them, that is). And as long as I remember that, I'm a serene machine, a patient pussycat, a forgiving feline, and a compassionate cat -- who's no longer afraid of life...or death, for that matter. Like BR, I look forward to joining my Higher Meower. (Just not yet.) But when I do, I believe I'll be back. And I fervently hope I'll be reincarnated as a BR, so I can pass on the knowledge I've been taught over the years to other Nathans who are eager to learn.

About The Author

Jacqueline L. Clarke has spent her career in the travel industry, first directing the development of advertising campaigns and sales promotion material for the U.S. Government's now defunct national tourist office, then as Vice President of Travel Programs for ENCORE, an international travel club, where she also served as editor of their bi-monthly travel magazine. Her most important achievement to date, however, has been learning to lead a spiritual life. And, as a result, today she is as capable of enjoying the companionship of other human beings as she is accepting the unconditional love of her two feline roommates, Bill and Bob.